Beholding Christ... The Lamb of God

A STUDY OF JOHN 15–21

BIBLE STUDY GUIDE

From the Bible-teaching ministry of

Charles R. Swindoll

INSIGHT FOR LIVING

Charles R. Swindoll is a graduate of Dallas Theological Seminary and has served in pastorates for more than twenty-four years, including churches in Texas, New England, and California. Since 1971 he has served as senior pastor of the First Evangelical Free Church of Fullerton, California. Chuck's radio program, "Insight for Living," began in 1979. In addition to his church and radio ministries, Chuck has written twenty-three books and numerous booklets on a variety of subjects.

Based on the outlines of Chuck's sermons, the study guide text is coauthored by Ken Gire, a graduate of Texas Christian University and Dallas Theological Seminary. The Living Insights are written by Bill Butterworth, a graduate of Florida Bible College, Dallas Theological Seminary, and Florida Atlantic University. Ken Gire is presently the director of educational products at Insight for Living, and Bill Butterworth is currently the director of counseling ministries.

Editor in Chief:	Cynthia Swindoll
Coauthor of Text:	Ken Gire
Author of Living Insights:	Bill Butterworth
Assistant Editor:	Karene Wells
Copy Manager:	Jac La Tour
Senior Copy Editor:	Jane Gillis
Copy Editor:	Kevin Moritz
Director, Communications Division:	Carla Beck
Project Manager:	Nina Paris
Project Supervisor:	Cassandra Clark
Art Director:	Donna Mayo
Production Artist:	Diana Vasquez
Typographer:	Bob Haskins
Calligrapher:	David Acquistapace
Cover:	Painting by S. Del Piambo, *Jesus Under the Burden of His Cross*
Print Production Manager:	Deedee Snyder
Printer:	Frye and Smith

Unless otherwise identified, all Scripture references are from the New American Standard Bible, © The Lockman Foundation 1960, 1962, 1963, 1968, 1971, 1972, 1973, 1975, 1977. Used by permission.

ISBN 0-8499-8297-9

Ordering Information

An album that contains sixteen messages on eight cassettes and corresponds to this study guide may be purchased through the Sales Department of Insight for Living, Post Office Box 4444, Fullerton, California 92634. For ordering information and a current catalog, please write our office or call (714) 870-9161.

Canadian residents may obtain a catalog and ordering information through Insight for Living Ministries, Post Office Box 2510, Vancouver, British Columbia, Canada V6B 3W7, (604) 272-5811. Australian residents should direct their correspondence to Insight for Living Ministries, General Post Office Box 2823 EE, Melbourne, Victoria 3001. Other overseas residents should direct their correspondence to our Fullerton office.

If you wish to order by Visa or MasterCard, you are welcome to use our toll-free number, (800) 772-8888, Monday through Friday, between the hours of 8:30 A.M. and 4:00 P.M., Pacific time. This number may be used anywhere in the United States except Alaska, California, and Hawaii. Orders from these areas can be made by calling our general office number, (714) 870-9161. Orders from Canada can be made by calling (604) 272-5811.

Table of Contents

Abiding 1

Qualities of a Friend 9

The Promise of Persecution 15

Functions of the Holy Spirit 23

Four Words That Keep Us Going 29

Divine Intercession 36

When Jesus Prayed for You 43

Arrest and Trial 50

Rush to Judgment 59

A Crack in the Rock 69

Death on a Cross 78

A Miraculous Resurrection 87

Reactions to the Resurrected Lord 94

Coming to Terms with Your Calling 100

"...And What about This Man?" 107

Many Other Signs...Many Other Things 116

Books for Probing Further 124

Acknowledgments 127

Ordering Information/Order Form 129

Beholding Christ . . .
The Lamb of God
A Study of John 15–21

John the Baptizer once introduced Christ as "the Lamb of God who takes away the sin of the world." Vivid words . . . true words.

In these concluding seven chapters of the Gospel of John, the Lamb is on display. After an intimate gathering with His men at their last supper together, He faces the horrors of six illegal trials, scourging, crucifixion, and death. The Lamb is slain. But the Lamb is later raised!

Even though some of this information is familiar to many Christians, we never tire of beholding the Lamb. I am delighted to know that you will be focusing your attention upon Him during these days. I hope each lesson will deepen your devotion for Christ, who accomplished our salvation at the cross . . . having been raised from the dead on our behalf.

Chuck Swindoll

Putting Truth into Action

Knowledge apart from application falls short of God's desire for His children. Knowledge must result in change and growth. Consequently, we have constructed this Bible study guide with these purposes in mind: (1) to stimulate discovery, (2) to increase understanding, and (3) to encourage application.

At the end of each lesson is a section called **Living Insights.** *There you'll be given assistance in further Bible study, and you'll be encouraged to contemplate and apply the things you've learned. This is the place where the lesson is fitted with shoe leather for your walk through the varied experiences of life.*

It's our hope that you'll discover numerous ways to use this tool. Some useful avenues we suggest are personal meditation, joint discovery, and discussion with your spouse, family, work associates, friends, or neighbors. The study guide is also practical for Sunday school classes, Bible study groups, and, of course, as a study aid for the "Insight for Living" radio broadcast.

In order to derive the greatest benefit from this process, we suggest that you record your responses to the lessons in the space which has been provided for you. In view of the kinds of questions asked, your study guide may become a journal filled with your many discoveries and commitments. We anticipate that you will find yourself returning to it periodically for review and encouragement.

Ken Gire

Ken Gire
Coauthor of Text

Bill Butterworth

Bill Butterworth
Author of Living Insights

Beholding Christ...
The Lamb of God

A STUDY OF JOHN 15–21

Abiding

John 15:1–11

A pair of scissors consists of two single blades. Yet the blades, regardless of how sharp or shiny, are useless without one essential element—the small metal screw that holds them together.

Can you imagine trying to cut some paper or fabric without that tiny screw? Of course, you could put a blade in each hand. But think of the effort and difficulty involved in trying to make an even, precise cut that way. But when that little screw brings both blades together, suddenly the cutting becomes effortless.

In our relationship with God, abiding in Jesus is the screw that holds everything together and makes us useful to Him.

In John 15, our Lord uses a similar homespun illustration—that of a vine and its branches—to teach His disciples the importance of fellowship with Him.

I. General Survey of John 15

Chapter 15 addresses the most important relationships a Christian must maintain. Verses 1–11 deal with the believer's relationship with Christ. The key term in this section of the chapter is *abide;* used ten times in these eleven verses, it emphasizes *union.* Verses 12–17 focus on the believer's relationship with other believers. *Love* is the key word in this section, used four times in the six verses; the emphasis here is on *communion.* Finally, verses 18–27 highlight the believer's relationship with the world. The key word is *hate,* used eight times in just ten verses. The emphasis of this last section is on *disunion.*

II. Specific Study of John 15:1–11

Moving from a bird's-eye view to a worm's-eye view, we'll examine verses 1–11 in greater detail.

A. Observations. Before we get into the interpretation of these verses, let's make a few preliminary observations.

1

1. **This entire passage is for believers only.** Jesus is talking intimately with His disciples, not the multitudes. His words are aimed at those who have already established a relationship with Him (see v. 3).
2. **The verses revolve around a metaphor.** The visual picture of the vine and branches tells us that the central idea is *vital union.* Just as the eagle and the stars and stripes are well-known American symbols, so the vineyard would have presented a familiar image to the Jews (compare Ps. 80:8–16; Isa. 5:1–7; Jer. 2:21; Ezek. 15, 19:10; Hos. 10:1).
3. **The main subject is abiding.** Jesus uses the image of fruit, not that of a seed taking root. The thrust of His teaching, therefore, is not on becoming a Christian but on becoming a *productive* Christian.
4. **The result of abiding is fruit bearing.** Scan the passage and note the following places where the word *fruit* is used: "does not bear fruit" (v. 2a); "bears fruit" (v. 2b); "bear more fruit" (v. 2c); "cannot bear fruit of itself" (v. 4); "bears much fruit" (v. 5); "bear much fruit" (v. 8). Fruit predominates this passage like a recurring motif in some still-life painting.

B. Interpretation. In the picture Jesus paints, three symbols stand out: the vine, the vinedresser, and the branch.

> "I am the true vine, and My Father is the vinedresser. Every branch in Me that does not bear fruit, He takes away; and every branch that bears fruit, He prunes it, that it may bear more fruit. You are already clean because of the word which I have spoken to you. Abide in Me, and I in you. As the branch cannot bear fruit of itself, unless it abides in the vine, so neither can you, unless you abide in Me." (vv. 1–4)

1. **The vine.** Jesus identifies Himself as the genuine vine—the only source of spiritual life. He is the one responsible for the fruit which we, as Christians, bear. Many view the fruit in John 15 as the result of evangelism, but in all probability it refers to character qualities of Christlikeness, namely, the fruit of the spirit: love, joy, peace, patience, kindness, goodness, faithfulness, gentleness, self-control (Gal. 5:22–23).[1]
2. **The vinedresser.** God the Father is pictured here as a busy, active, faithful gardener, working in His vineyard—an image already well-established in the Old Testament.

---

1. Fruit is a part of the tree and serves to identify what type of tree it is. According to verse 4, one cannot bear fruit without abiding in the vine. However, evangelism *can* take place through people not abiding in Christ (Phil. 1:15–18).

Let me sing now for my well-beloved
A song of my beloved concerning His vineyard.
My well-beloved had a vineyard on a fertile hill.
And He dug it all around, removed its stones,
And planted it with the choicest vine.
And He built a tower in the middle of it,
And hewed out a wine vat in it;
Then He expected it to produce good grapes,
But it produced only worthless ones.
"And now, O inhabitants of Jerusalem and men of
    Judah,
Judge between Me and My vineyard.
What more was there to do for My vineyard that
    I have not done in it?
Why, when I expected it to produce good grapes
    did it produce worthless ones?..."
For the vineyard of the Lord of hosts is the house
    of Israel,
And the men of Judah His delightful plant.
Thus He looked for justice, but behold, blood-
    shed;
For righteousness, but behold, a cry of distress.
    (Isa. 5:1–4, 7)

Jesus probably had this passage in mind when He talked of
His Father being the vinedresser. In John 15:2, Jesus reveals
two actions of the vinedresser: one, He does something with
the branch that isn't bearing *any* fruit at all; two, He does
something with the branch that isn't bearing *enough* fruit.
In the first case, He "takes away"; in the second, He "prunes."
Vines occasionally yield an unproductive, fruitless branch.
When that happens, the gardener immediately goes to work,
as Merrill Tenney notes in his commentary.

> Viticulture...consists mainly of pruning. In
> pruning a vine, two principles are generally ob-
> served: first, all dead wood must be ruthlessly
> removed; and second, the live wood must be cut
> back drastically. Dead wood harbors insects and
> disease and may cause the vine to rot, to say
> nothing of being unproductive and unsightly. Live
> wood must be trimmed back in order to prevent
> such heavy growth that the life of the vine goes
> into the wood rather than into fruit. The vine-
> yards in the early spring look like a collection of
> barren, bleeding stumps; but in the fall they are

3

filled with luxuriant purple grapes. As the farmer wields the pruning knife on his vines, so God cuts dead wood out from among His saints, and often cuts back the living wood so far that His method seems cruel. Nevertheless, from those who have suffered the most there often comes the greatest fruitfulness.[2]

The Pain of Being Pruned

For the plant, pruning is never a pleasant experience. Yet without it, the vine would wind up a tangle of unproductive overgrowth.

Is God pruning your life now? If so, it can be a painful process, and you will probably bleed more sap than you will produce fruit. But if your branches are smarting from the sharp swings of God's pruning hook, take hope. Just as there is a time to be pruned, so there is a time to be productive. And that is only a short growing season away!

---

3. **The branch.** Jesus uses the figure of the branch to depict the Christian. In verse 2, He makes an important distinction between our position in the vine, which is Christ, and our production. The difference is seen when comparing verse 2 with verse 4: "Every branch in Me" speaks of our position in Christ; "Abide in Me" is a command given to those who are already branches. This distinction separates the two activities of the believer: the *active* responsibility of abiding—our *position* (v. 4)—and the *passive* response of bearing fruit— our *production* (v. 5). Note that the command is not to produce fruit but to abide. When we are abiding, fruit comes naturally. The fruit in view here is not produced by the branch but by the vine itself. Without abiding, a branch cannot produce even a bud of real fruit.

> "I am the vine, you are the branches; he who
> abides in Me, and I in him, he bears much fruit;
> for apart from Me you can do nothing." (v. 5)

Nothing? That's right, nothing ... at least nothing of genuine or eternal value. Whatever you produce in your life that is not an outgrowth of a vital relationship with Christ is like plastic fruit. It looks good from a distance but can't bear up

---

2. Merrill C. Tenney, *John: The Gospel of Belief* (Grand Rapids, Mich.: William B. Eerdmans Publishing Co., 1948), pp. 227–28.

under the close scrutiny of eternity. And what about the far-reaching effects of not abiding? Verse 6 describes the charring consequences.

> "If anyone does not abide in Me, he is thrown
> away as a branch, and dries up; and they gather
> them, and cast them into the fire, and they are
> burned."

If we abide in Christ, we bear fruit; if we don't, we become barren. And as a barren branch, we become useless to those around us, either for shade or for nourishment. When the vineyard is in this condition, the vinedresser comes in and cleans it up with His disciplinary hand. But He doesn't take away our salvation, only our reward.[3] The original Greek in verse 6 is definite: the Christian who lives in the power of the flesh is thrown away as "a branch." The believer never ceases to be a branch, no matter how barren that branch becomes. And furthermore, the Father does not put the branch in the fire, but the works done in the power of the flesh. Note that the plural *them* could not refer to the singular *branch*. Logically, it must refer to the works done in the flesh by the believer. And it is these works—not the believer—that are burned up. Paul conveys the same truth through a different metaphor in 1 Corinthians 3:12–15.

> Now if any man builds upon the foundation with
> gold, silver, precious stones, wood, hay, straw,
> each man's work will become evident; for the
> day will show it, because it is to be revealed with
> fire; and the fire itself will test the quality of each
> man's work. If any man's work which he has built
> upon it remains, he shall receive a reward. If any
> man's work is burned up, he shall suffer loss; but
> he himself shall be saved, yet so as through fire.

Most of our lives are mixtures of wood, hay, and straw, along with gold, silver, and precious stones. The former, God destroys; the latter, He blesses. Verses 7–11 delineate those blessings. The first is that *prayer is answered.*

> "If you abide in Me, and My words abide in you,
> ask whatever you wish, and it shall be done for
> you." (v. 7)

---

3. For a clear discussion that reconciles many of the problem passages that seem to imply believers can lose their salvation, see *Grace in Eclipse: A Study on Eternal Rewards,* by Zane Clark Hodges (Dallas, Tex.: Redencíon Viva, 1985) and *The Gospel Under Siege,* also by Hodges (Dallas, Tex.: Redencíon Viva, 1981).

The second is that *God is glorified.*

> "By this is My Father glorified, that you bear much fruit, and so prove to be My disciples." (v. 8)

The third is that *your life will be motivated by love.*

> "Just as the Father has loved Me, I have also loved you; abide in My love. If you keep My commandments, you will abide in My love; just as I have kept My Father's commandments, and abide in His love." (vv. 9–10)

The fourth is that *joy will be yours in abundance.* Like a flag that flies over the castle when the king is on the throne, so joy will stand over your life as a testimony that Jesus reigns in your heart.

> "These things I have spoken to you, that My joy may be in you, and that your joy may be made full." (v. 11)

III. Practical and Personal Summary

Two important truths stem from this study: first, *refusing to abide results in barrenness;* and second, *abiding results in fruitfulness.* Abiding in Christ should be as natural as a tree abiding in the soil— and as necessary! When the tree faithfully abides in that soil, fruit is the inevitable result. And like the person who abides in the Word, as described by the psalmist, so is the person who abides in Christ.

> And he will be like a tree firmly planted by streams of water,
> Which yields its fruit in its season,
> And its leaf does not wither;
> And in whatever he does, he prospers. (Ps. 1:3)

🐢 *Living Insights*

Study One ▬▬▬▬▬▬▬▬▬▬▬▬▬▬▬▬▬▬▬▬▬▬▬▬▬▬▬▬

There is no better way to behold Christ than to study the Gospel of John. In order to get a feel for the seven chapters we will be studying together, let's conduct a little overview of John 15–21.

• Take a few minutes to skim these chapters. As you read, record your observations about Christ. What do you notice about Him?

Beholding Christ: John 15–21	
Passages	Observations

Continued on next page

Living Insights

The focus of our opening study has been abiding. The natural result of abiding is fruit bearing. Can you think of some specific examples of fruit in your life?

- Think through this issue. Do you see evidence that you are in Christ? Write down specific, recent examples of fruit in your life.

Fruit in My Life

_____

_____

_____

_____

_____

_____

_____

_____

_____

_____

_____

_____

_____

_____

_____

_____

_____

_____

_____

_____

_____

Qualities of a Friend
John 15:12–17

Born of older parents in eighteenth-century Devonshire, England, the famous poet Samuel Taylor Coleridge was a lonely genius. When his father died, nine-year-old Coleridge was sent to London to live with his uncle. There he entered the charity school of Christ's Hospital, taking refuge in books as his only friends.

At nineteen, he entered Cambridge, where his career interests vacillated between medicine, philosophy, and writing. He quickly distinguished himself as a scholar and gained notoriety as a poet, critic, and playwright. Even in his twenties, Coleridge lectured extensively on Shakespeare and Milton. Many of his poems—such as "The Nightingale," "Kubla Kahn," and the "Rime of the Ancient Mariner"—became classics.

But none of these achievements satisfied the emptiness in his heart for friendship. By the age of twenty-four, he had turned to drugs to deaden the resounding loneliness. His only deep friendships were with fellow poet William Wordsworth and later with physician James Gillman, who cared for Coleridge in his early forties. For the last eighteen years of his life, years that in many ways were his happiest, Coleridge rarely left the Gillman home.

Most of Coleridge's works dwell on misery, tragedy, and the barrenness of life . . . except for one poem written shortly before his death, titled "Youth and Age." The second stanza cradles the moving line: "Friendship is a sheltering tree."[1]

In the gray twilight of his life, Coleridge recognized something that genius, popularity, and money could never replace—the value of a friend.

I. A Study of the Second Section of John 15

When death nears, it is remarkable how important the shade of our sheltering friends becomes. Not even the Son of God wanted to be alone when the shadow of the cross darkened His last days. At that time, more than any other, He wanted to be surrounded by His most intimate friends. And with those friends Jesus shared the innermost feelings of His heart in what is known as the Upper Room Discourse. Today, we will look at the second section of John 15, verses 12–17, where Christ discusses the love and communion believers should have with one another.

A. Transitional connection: the command. Jesus has just told the disciples, " 'Abide in My love' " (v. 9b). The subject of love is the transitional bridge between two pools of thought: love for

---

1. As quoted by John Bartlett, *Familiar Quotations,* 14th ed., rev. and enl., ed. Emery Morison Beck (Boston, Mass.: Little, Brown and Co., 1980), p. 527.

Him and love for one another. Now, He broaches the subject of their relationship with each other.

> "This is My commandment, that you love one another,
> just as I have loved you. . . . This I command you, that
> you love one another." (vv. 12, 17)

1. **The content.** The verb in verse 12 is in the present tense. It indicates ongoing action: "keep on loving one another." Jesus' point is that love is not to be a sporadic, impulsive, or capricious outburst of emotion; it is to be a sustained, intense, and committed outworking of the will. Love is not a Christmas feeling that bubbles to the surface when circumstances are conducive; it is a decision to continually seek the highest good of others. Its roots are not in humanism or in Hollywood, but in heaven. We aren't to love others on the basis of their inherent goodness or external attractiveness, but on the basis of the example Jesus set for us.

2. **The comparison.** Up until this time, Jesus has taught us to love our neighbors as ourselves (Luke 10:27). Our love for ourselves has been the basis of comparison for our love for others. But now He gives the disciples a new commandment based on a different point of comparison. They are to love one another " 'just as I have loved you.' " Jesus loved the disciples unconditionally. He loved them in their unbelief (Matt. 14:31); He loved them in their pettiness (18:1–6); He loved them in their desertion (26:31). He loved them in their denial (26:33–34); He loved them in their laziness (26:36–46); He loved them in their betrayal (26:47–50). And He loved them to the end (John 13:1). Jesus could continually love the disciples because He continually abided in the Father, vitally linked in unbroken fellowship. Now as we come to verse 13 of John 15, we see their relationship move to a deeper level—beyond discipleship to friendship.

B. **Essential characteristics: the qualities.** As He introduces this new level of relating, Jesus makes the qualities of a friend visible by detailing four massive limbs of that "sheltering tree."

1. **Disregard for personal sacrifice.** The first branch of the tree is found in verse 13.

> "Greater love has no one than this, that one lay
> down his life for his friends."

The primary interpretation of verse 13 refers to Christ laying down His life for the disciples. But on a secondary level, there's a principle that relates to friendship. When you have a friend, you will disregard the pain of personal sacrifice— even if that sacrifice is death.

Charles Dickens's *Tale of Two Cities* presents a classic illustration of John 15:13. Set during the French Revolution, it is the story of two friends, Charles Darnay and Sydney Carton. Darnay is a young Frenchman who has been thrown in a dungeon to await the guillotine. Carton is a wasted English lawyer whose life has been one of careless reprobation.

In a beautiful allegory of Christ's atonement for us, Carton slips into the dungeon and exchanges clothes with the prisoner, allowing Darnay to escape. The next morning, Sydney Carton makes his way up the steps that lead to the guillotine. His final words are triumphant:

> "I see the lives for which I lay down my life,
> peaceful, useful, prosperous and happy, in
> that England which I shall see no more....
> It is a far, far better thing that I do, than I
> have ever done; it is a far, far better rest
> that I go to than I have ever known."[2]

That is true friendship. That is the love Jesus demonstrated to His disciples—and offers to you and me (Rom. 5:8). No wonder the hymn says, "What a friend we have in Jesus."

2. **Dedication to mutual aims.** The second large limb in friendship's sheltering tree is found in verse 14.

> "You are My friends, if you do what I command
> you."

The present tense here—meaning "keep on doing"—tells us that friendship depends on common aims and outlook. In this case, Jesus' goals became those of the disciples, revealing the friendship that existed between them. We find another example of this quality in the friendship between Paul and Timothy.

> But I hope in the Lord Jesus to send Timothy to
> you shortly, so that I also may be encouraged
> when I learn of your condition. For I have no one
> else of kindred spirit who will genuinely be concerned for your welfare. For they all seek after
> their own interests, not those of Christ Jesus. But
> you know of his proven worth that he served

2. Charles Dickens, *A Tale of Two Cities* (Garden City, N.Y.: Nelson Doubleday, n.d.), pp. 350–51.

with me in the furtherance of the gospel like a
child serving his father. (Phil. 2:19–22)

We see two important things in these verses: a statement
and an analogy. Verse 20 contains the statement: "I have no
one else of kindred spirit." The Greek word, used only here
in all the New Testament, means "equal soul" or "like soul."
Aristotle once said: "A true friend is one soul in two bodies."[3]
That is how close Paul and Timothy were—with a one-
souled quality only true friends have. In verse 22, we find
the analogy: "He served *with* me in the furtherance of the
gospel like a child serving his father" (emphasis added). In
friendship there's a union of philosophy, a mutuality of aims
and objectives, a kinship of souls.

3. **Discussion of privileged information.** A third bough
branching in friendship's sheltering tree grows from verse 15
of John 15.

"No longer do I call you slaves, for the slave does
not know what his master is doing; but I have
called you friends, for all things that I have heard
from My Father I have made known to you."

In the slave-master relationship there's only one common
ground—work.

The slave could never be a partner. The slave
was defined in Greek law as *a living tool.* His
master never opened his mind to him; the slave
had to do what he was told without reason and
without explanation.[4]

But not so in a friendship: " 'All things . . . I have made known
to you' " (v. 15). Open sharing, nothing hidden, no super-
ficiality. Real friendship is marked by the sharing of soul
secrets. But notice the context of this intimate sharing. It is
not public information traded on the lips of indiscreet on-
lookers; it is shared in the private setting of the upper room
to a select, trusted few.

Friends of the King

The courts of eastern kings held an elite group of
men called "friends of the king." They had unrestricted
access to the monarch. Having the right to even come

---

3. *Five Thousand Quotations for All Occasions,* ed. Lewis C. Henry (Garden City, N.Y.: Doubleday and Co., 1945), p. 101.

4. William Barclay, *The Gospel of John,* vol. 2, The Daily Study Bible Series (Edinburgh,
Scotland: Saint Andrew Press, 1956), pp. 208–9.

> into the king's bedchamber, they often met with him informally before he saw his political, economic, or military advisors. Think about the incredible offer Jesus gives—to be no longer slaves but friends. We need no longer gaze at Him from afar. We are no longer excluded from His intimate circle of confidants. Friends! Incredible, but true.

4. **Desire to implement fulfillment.** This fourth branch of friendship is found in verse 16, where Jesus' goal was to help the disciples achieve maximum productivity.

> "You did not choose Me, but I chose you, and appointed you, that you should go and bear fruit, and that your fruit should remain, that whatever you ask of the Father in My name, He may give to you."

Jesus reached out and chose each disciple and purposely committed Himself to their finding fulfillment. Nothing is more exciting than seeing a close friend succeed. And that should be the purpose of our relationships—to help each other reach maximum fulfillment.

II. A Summary of Today's Truths

Before you walk away from this study, fix two truths in your mind. One, a sheltering tree bears the fruit of security, confidence, care, and encouragement. Two, a sheltering tree has roots that abide. Friendship lends warmth and meaning to life. Let's not live in such a way that Coleridge's self-written epitaph might apply to us:

> Beneath this sod
> A poet lies, or that which once seemed he—
> Oh, lift a thought in prayer for S.T.C.!
> That he, who many a year, with toil of breath,
> Found death in life, may here find life in death.[5]

Let's live our lives under the sheltering tree of Christ's friendship, where the fruit from His spreading branches can nourish and refresh us forever.

Continued on next page

---

5. Samuel Taylor Coleridge, as quoted by Bartlett, *Familiar Quotations,* p. 530.

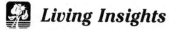 *Living Insights*

Most of us have been richly blessed by God with special friends. One of the most famous friendships in Scripture is the relationship between David and Jonathan. Let's dust off the pages of the Old Testament and rediscover this heartwarming story.

● The story of Jonathan and David is found in 1 Samuel 18 and 19. Read these two chapters and jot down the qualities that made this such a unique friendship.

Qualities of a Friendship

Reference   Quality

_____   _____

_____   _____

_____   _____

_____   _____

_____   _____

_____   _____

_____   _____

Living Insights

Whom do you consider your best friend? Does this person know of this special honor? Have you been communicating appreciation for this friendship? Let's take some time to do that now.

● Do something to communicate your appreciation to your best friend, maybe with a note, a phone call, or a visit. Or even with a gift—perhaps a book by his favorite author or a bouquet of her favorite flowers. But remember, it really is the thought that counts.

The Promise of Persecution
John 15:18–16:4

"When Christ calls a man, he bids him come and die."[1] Those were the uncompromising words of the young German pastor Dietrich Bonhoeffer. Resolutely standing up for his faith, Bonhoeffer delivered a lecture over the Berlin airwaves in February 1933 in which he castigated the German public for craving a political idol. That idol was Adolf Hitler.

Before he could finish his broadcast, Bonhoeffer was abruptly cut off, a fateful foreshadowing of things to come. Refusing to compromise his Christian principles, Bonhoeffer resisted the pervasive influence of Nazism. That resistance led to his imprisonment in April 1943 and ultimately to his death. John W. Doberstein relates the incident.

> In the gray dawn of an April day in 1945, in the concentration camp at Flossenburg, shortly before it was liberated by the allied forces, Dietrich Bonhoeffer was executed by special order of Heinrich Himmler.... For innumerable Christians in Germany, on the Continent, in England, and in America, Dietrich Bonhoeffer's death has been a contemporary confirmation of Tertullian's dictum, "The blood of the martyrs is the seed of the Church."[2]

The Christian life is a road paved with the sharp stones of persecution—a truth taught and exemplified by Christ Himself, as we shall see in our lesson for today.

I. Persecution: General Predictions from Scripture

As we page through the New Testament, the blood of martyrs stains our fingertips. Paul's life is a good example. Acts 9:15–16 predicts the suffering he would endure for Christ, the fulfillment of which can be found in 1 Corinthians 4:11–13 and 2 Corinthians 4:8–9. And as Hebrews 11:36–38 reveals, Paul serves as a *typical* example of the Christian experience, not an exception.

> And others experienced mockings and scourgings, yes, also chains and imprisonment. They were stoned, they were sawn in two, they were tempted, they were put to death with the sword; they went about in sheepskins, in goatskins, being destitute, afflicted, ill-treated (men of whom the world was not worthy), wandering in deserts and mountains and caves and holes in the ground.

---

1. Dietrich Bonhoeffer, *Life Together,* trans. John W. Doberstein (New York, N.Y.: Harper and Row, Publishers, 1954), p. 8.

2. Bonhoeffer, *Life Together,* p. 7.

In describing the last times, Paul peers over the centuries and issues a warning to the ones standing on the threshold of those times.

> But realize this, that in the last days difficult times will come. For men will be lovers of self, lovers of money, boastful, arrogant, revilers, disobedient to parents, ungrateful, unholy, unloving, irreconcilable, malicious gossips, without self-control, brutal, haters of good, treacherous, reckless, conceited, lovers of pleasure rather than lovers of God; holding to a form of godliness, although they have denied its power; and avoid such men as these. (2 Tim. 3:1–5)

Although we don't claim it as readily as we do other Scripture verses, persecution is part and parcel to the promises of God.

> But you followed my teaching, conduct, purpose, faith, patience, love, perseverance, persecutions, and sufferings, such as happened to me at Antioch, at Iconium and at Lystra; what persecutions I endured, and out of them all the Lord delivered me! And indeed, all who desire to live godly in Christ Jesus will be persecuted. (2 Tim. 3:10–12)

Yet behind the clouds of persecution brooding on the horizon, an indomitable sun shines, piercing the gloom with a triumphant ray of hope.

> "These things I have spoken to you, that in Me you may have peace. In the world you have tribulation, but take courage; I have overcome the world." (John 16:33)

II. Persecution: Specific Instructions from Jesus

As we turn to John 15, we find that Jesus gives some pointed instructions regarding persecution.

A. Who will persecute? Verse 18 overshadows verse 17 like an eclipse. The sun shines brightly in verse 17 as Jesus talks to His disciples about their love for one another. Then suddenly the word *hate* is introduced, a thought that obstructs the previous conversation and darkens the mood in the upper room.

> "If the world hates you, you know that it has hated Me before it hated you. If you were of the world, the world would love its own; but because you are not of the world, but I chose you out of the world, therefore the world hates you." (vv. 18–19)[3]

The first source of persecution Jesus cites is the world, or *kosmos.* Biblically speaking, the *kosmos* is not the earth, per se, but the world system—that ravenous lion garbed in the sophisticated

---

3. In verse 18, the word *if* should be translated "since" because the syntax of the original Greek does not indicate contingency but certainty.

sheepskin of culture, religion, politics, and education. Like Hitler, the world embraces those who follow its philosophy but persecutes those, like Bonhoeffer, who resist it. In 16:2, Jesus becomes more specific in identifying the persecutors.

"They will make you outcasts from the synagogue, but an hour is coming for everyone who kills you to think that he is offering service to God."

From legalistic Pharisees to liberal pastors, persecution from the world has often emanated from the religious sector (see Matt. 23:29–35).

B. What can be expected? We can first expect the world to show us hate (John 15:19).[4] Wearing many faces, this emotion ranges from indifference to indignation, from avoidance to animosity. And these faces can glare at you from your family, your classmates, your business associates, your neighbors, and yes, even religious people . . . possibly from within your own church. Verse 20 indicates we can then expect persecution.

"Remember the word that I said to you, 'A slave is not greater than his master.' If they persecuted Me, they will also persecute you; if they kept My word, they will keep yours also."

There it is in black and white: the promise of persecution. The Greek term translated *persecute* means "to put to flight, to pursue." New Testament scholar A. T. Robertson says the word means "to chase like a wild beast."[5] And strange as it may seem, persecuting Christians has run more rampant and ravenous during the twentieth century than it did during the first. Much of this persecution takes place behind the Iron Curtain, declares a leader of the underground church.

As a member of the Underground Church who has survived and escaped, I have brought you a message, an appeal, a plea from my brethren whom I have left behind. . . . Behind the walls of the Iron Curtain the drama, bravery and martyrdom of the Early Church is happening all over again—now—and the free Church sleeps.[6]

4. An explanation of the hatred toward Christians in the first century is given by William Barclay in *The Gospel of John,* vol. 2, The Daily Study Bible Series (Edinburgh, Scotland: Saint Andrew Press, 1956), pp. 214–17.

5. A. T. Robertson, *Word Pictures in the New Testament,* vol. 5 (Nashville, Tenn.: Broadman Press, 1932), p. 262.

6. Richard Wurmbrand, *Tortured for Christ* (Basingstoke, United Kingdom: Lakeland, 1983), pp. 127–28. Other books that document this persecution are *God's Smuggler* by Brother Andrew (Old Tappan, N.J.: Fleming H. Revell Co., 1968) and *Remember the Prisoners,* ed. Peter Masters (Chicago, Ill.: Moody Press, 1986).

With the pervasive spread of communism throughout the world, the church of tomorrow could very well be the underground church. Verse 2 of chapter 16, quoted earlier, informs us of the last thing we can expect from the world, and that is death—"everyone who kills you." It has happened since the first century, is happening now, and will continue in greater measure as the last times draw near.

C. Why will it occur? Jesus gives us three reasons why persecution will occur.

   1. **"Because you are not of the world"** (15:19). The world wants conformity. It has a certain pattern or mold that it expects everyone to fit into (see Rom. 12:2). It loves those who fit the mold and hates those who don't. And if we don't fit the mold, one of two things will happen: either we will break the mold or the mold will break us. The best example of this is Daniel, who was indicted and thrown into the lions' den because he refused to let his worldly peers pressure his principles (Dan. 6:1–9).

   2. **"Because they do not know the One who sent Me"** (John 15:21; compare 16:2). Beneath its superficial surface, the world seethes in a turbulent cauldron of unbelief, resulting in resentment toward those who walk in the truth. An exemplary life rebukes everyone it comes in contact with; consequently, it stirs up a hornets' nest of emotions.

   3. **"That the word may be fulfilled"** (15:25). The very existence of Christians in the world produces guilt for many people. In verses 22–24, Jesus, in effect, is saying: "If I hadn't come, the world wouldn't even be aware of its sin. But because I'm here, they're painfully aware, and that's the reason they hate Me."

      It is in fact dangerous to be good. The classic instance of that is the fate which befell Aristides in Athens. He was called Aristides the Just; and yet he was banished. When one of the citizens was asked why he had voted for the banishment of Aristides, he answered: "Because I am tired of hearing him always called the Just." That was why men killed Socrates; they called him the human gadfly. He was always compelling men to think and to examine themselves, and men hated that and hated him and killed him.[7]

7. Barclay, *The Gospel of John,* pp. 216–17.

Why Don't We Face More Persecution Today?

Maybe we don't experience more persecution in our own lives because we blend in too well with the crowd. Take Jonas Hanaway, for example. Hanaway tried to introduce the umbrella into society when walking the streets of England one day. But nobody had ever seen an umbrella before. Because he stood out so much from the crowds around him, they pelted him with stones and dirt.

Today, an umbrella is a common possession for most people. It is universally accepted in all social and professional circles. But that has not always been the case.

Maybe we've gone the way of the umbrella and lost our uniqueness as Christians. If the verse is true that the godly will suffer persecution, then maybe, just maybe, our lives don't stand out enough to attract anybody's attention . . . let alone anybody's persecution.

D. How should we react? Our reaction to persecution should be one of acceptance, as 1 Peter 4:12 instructs.

> Beloved, do not be surprised at the fiery ordeal among you, which comes upon you for your testing, as though some strange thing were happening to you.

Back in the book of John, Jesus gives us four suggestions on how to react, two negative and two positive, that will help us keep our bearings when persecution starts to bewilder us.

1. Positively. First, *we should rely on the Holy Spirit.* Almost abruptly, the Holy Spirit is introduced in verse 26 of chapter 15.

> "When the Helper comes, whom I will send to you from the Father, that is the Spirit of truth, who proceeds from the Father, He will bear witness of Me."

Why is the Holy Spirit introduced at this juncture? Because He is the Helper—the *paraklētos,* the "one called alongside" to strengthen and support us. It is the Holy Spirit who gives us our sea legs during the storms of persecution. He's the one who keeps us from falling on our faces or getting washed overboard altogether. Second, *we should stand firm and boldly testify of our faith in Christ.*

> "And you will bear witness also, because you have been with Me from the beginning." (v. 27)

When persecuted, we tend to back off and retreat rather than stand firm in our faith.

2. Negatively. First, *we shouldn't stumble.*

> "These things I have spoken to you, that you may
> be kept from stumbling." (16:1)

The Greek word for "stumble" is *skandalizō.* From it we get our word *scandal.* When you stumble, your walk is interrupted, and that is what the Lord is trying to prevent. Second, *we shouldn't forget.* We Christians are notorious for remembering what we ought to forget and forgetting what we ought to remember, aren't we? To help us break this habit, Jesus ties verse 4 around our finger:

> "But these things I have spoken to you, that when
> their hour comes, you may remember that I told
> you of them. And these things I did not say to you
> at the beginning, because I was with you." (v. 4)

III. Persecution: Personal Application for Christians

As we walk away from this lesson, let's take three applications with us.

A. There is a great difference between picking a fight and enduring persecution. Some members in the family of God are abrasive and have an unusual penchant for rubbing people the wrong way. They start a fight; and when people hit back, they rationalize it by saying that the failure to hear truth is just another sign of the end times. Paul's words have great significance on this very point: "If possible, so far as it depends on you, be at peace with all men" (Rom. 12:18).

B. There is a great difference between loving the world and living in the world. It's not the Lord's plan to take us out of the world but to give us protection during the pilgrimage: " 'I do not ask Thee to take them out of the world, but to keep them from the evil one' " (John 17:15). God doesn't want us living on the mountaintop, although He occasionally takes us there for fellowship. He wants us in the valley, where the people are. But He wants us there as pilgrims, not settlers. For the world is a battleground, not a playground.

C. There is a great difference between running scared and being informed. The prophetic clock is synchronized with God's time. Unhurried by wars and rumors of wars, it ticks steadily forward at its own pace, with its own schedules to keep. The Lord has seen fit to reveal some of the details, not to frighten us, but to fuel our faith (see Matt. 24).

Divine Help in the Face of Persecution

In his letters from prison, which were smuggled out by sympathetic German guards, Dietrich Bonhoeffer had these

---

reassuring words to say about persecution—words we all can benefit from today.

I believe that God will give us all the strength we need to help us to resist in all time of distress. But he never gives it in advance, lest we should rely on ourselves and not on him alone. A faith such as this should allay all our fears for the future.[8]

Living Insights

Study One

Before we close the book on the fifteenth chapter of John, let's take one last look at its great teaching. These twenty-seven verses are packed with truth, love, and power.

- A good way to extract all you can from a text is by paraphrasing, or putting the passage in your own words. If you've never done this before, John 15 is an excellent place to start! You'll soon discover how you are able to amplify the meanings and emotions of the chapter. Don't be in a hurry. If you are unable to do all the verses, that's OK. Do as much as time will allow.

My Paraphrase of John 15

_____

_____

_____

_____

_____

_____

_____

_____

_____

Continued on next page

8. Dietrich Bonhoeffer, *Letters and Papers from Prison,* enl. ed., ed. Eberhard Bethge (New York, N.Y.: Macmillan Co., 1972), p. 11.

_____

_____

_____

_____

_____

_____

_____

_____

_____

_____

_____

Living Insights

Study Two

This chapter tells us bluntly, If you live a godly life, you'll face some persecution! Can you relate? Have you run into your share of resistance when you've tried to do what's right? You are not alone. It might be rather eye-opening to talk with a group of friends or family members about their experiences. Use the following questions as conversation starters and encourage each person to share.

• What was the situation?
• Who provided the persecution?
• Why did it occur?
• How did you react?
• What did you learn from it?

Functions of the Holy Spirit
John 16:4–15

Saying good-bye is never easy, whether it's at an airport, a family reunion, or the deathbed of a loved one. The Last Supper was no exception. For Jesus and His disciples, this was their last meal together.

Like shorn sheep shivering in the chill of the evening, the disciples huddled near their shepherd that night—fearful, saddened, grieved. And good shepherd that He was, Jesus took them in His arms to reassure them that He wouldn't leave them as orphans (John 14:18).

The single, most important message Jesus wanted to communicate was that His presence would be replaced with that of the Holy Spirit. The disciples understood little of what Jesus said about the Spirit that night, but within a few weeks the reality of His words would transform their lives. In this lesson, we want to discover some of the functions of the Holy Spirit—functions as active and vital today as they were in the first century.

I. Message from the Savior
At that last supper Jesus ate with His disciples, He had many things to say. But mainly He wanted them to know two secrets—one about Himself, the other about themselves.

A. The secret of His victorious life. Time and again throughout the Upper Room Discourse Jesus referred to the vital union He had with the Father. He wanted to impress upon the disciples that the Father was *in Him* and that He was *in the Father.*

B. The secret of their victorious life. Jesus' relationship with the Father was to serve as an example to the disciples of their new relationship with the Spirit. Just as Jesus had a vital union with the Father, so the disciples were to have a vital union with the Holy Spirit. They were to draw upon the Spirit's power as Jesus had drawn upon the Father's. And just as the Father was in Jesus, so the Spirit would be in them—empowering, illuminating, and comforting.

II. Ministry of the Spirit
Reading John 13–16, it's easy to see the panic growing within each disciple. In chapter 13, Jesus tells the disciples that they can't go with Him. In chapter 14, He hints at a persecution to come. Like abandoned children, the disciples suddenly feel insecure. Realizing this, Jesus explains in detail exactly how the Spirit will minister to them.

A. The reaction of the disciples. The disciples' need for support is seen in verses 4–6 of chapter 16.

> "But these things I have spoken to you, that when
> their hour comes, you may remember that I told you
> of them. And these things I did not say to you at the
> beginning, because I was with you. But now I am
> going to Him who sent Me; and none of you asks Me,
> 'Where are You going?' But because I have said these
> things to you, sorrow has filled your heart."

Between the lines of these verses is a truth most of us hate to
admit: we have a basic need to be held securely, to be kept. For
over three years the Lord has "kept" the disciples. But now He
is leaving, and they are so distraught that they're speechless
(v. 5) and filled with sorrow (v. 6). The Greek term for *sorrow*
means "grief," and, indeed, they grieve like bereaved children
who have just been separated from their parents.

B. The solution of Christ. Moved by their insecurity, Jesus
assures the disciples with these words.

> "But I tell you the truth, it is to your advantage that
> I go away; for if I do not go away, the Helper shall
> not come to you; but if I go, I will send Him to you."
> (v. 7)

The word *advantage* means "profitable" in the original Greek.
It's hard to believe that Jesus' absence could be profitable or
advantageous for the disciples and for us, but it's true. Why?
Because Jesus would send a divine Helper in His place. And how
would that be an advantage? As long as Jesus was on the earth
in His physical body, He could only be in one place at one time,
but the Spirit could strengthen each of them at the same time
because He would work from *within.* In the innermost recesses
of their hearts where there was panic, He would bring peace.
And where there was fear, He would bring fortitude.

C. The functions of the Holy Spirit. In verses 8–11, three
specific functions of the Spirit convict the world *through* the
believer.

> "And He, when He comes, will convict the world con-
> cerning sin, and righteousness, and judgment; con-
> cerning sin, because they do not believe in Me; and
> concerning righteousness, because I go to the Father,
> and you no longer behold Me; and concerning judg-
> ment, because the ruler of this world has been judged."

  1. "Concerning sin" (v. 9). The Spirit uses the faithful, loving
Christian as a visual aid to convict the unbeliever (see 1 Cor.
7:12–14). Our responsibility is to love Christ and faithfully
follow Him, not to bring conviction. That's the Spirit's job.

2. **"Concerning righteousness"** (v. 10). The believer should have a standard, or lifestyle, foreign to the unsaved person. Since the world can no longer see the righteousness of Jesus, they can only see it reflected off us—like the moon reflects the brightness of the unseen sun. When nothing eclipses our relationship with Christ, we will reflect a beautiful light to a world shrouded in darkness.

3. **"Concerning judgment"** (v. 11). Reading verse 11, we naturally assume that the future Judgment is in view. But such is not the case. The world is convicted because a judgment has already taken place: " 'the ruler of this world *has been* judged' " (emphasis added). When unbelievers, who live under that ruler, witness the believer's free and unfettered life, the Holy Spirit shows them that their ruler has no power over the saint. And, in seeing that, they realize that a judgment has taken place. Their ruler stands condemned; consequently, so do they. The disciples' minds are reeling by now, so Jesus cuts His sermon short.

> "I have many more things to say to you, but you cannot bear them now." (v. 12)

In verses 8–11, Jesus revealed the functions of the Spirit through the believer; but now, in verses 13–15, He reveals the Holy Spirit's ministry *to* the believer. The first function can be seen in verse 13.

> "But when He, the Spirit of truth, comes, He will guide you into all the truth; for He will not speak on His own initiative, but whatever He hears, He will speak; and He will disclose to you what is to come."

The Holy Spirit teaches us the written truth of God, which He clarifies but does not originate: " 'whatever He hears, He will speak.' " Meaning what? Meaning that He speaks the thoughts that come from the depths of God's mind (1 Cor. 2:9–13). But this raises an important question: How can we be sure that the teaching we receive is really from God? John 16:14 answers that question.

> "He shall glorify Me; for He shall take of Mine, and shall disclose it to you."

The Holy Spirit glorifies the Son of God. He neither diminishes the Son's glory nor steals the spotlight for Himself. When the Holy Spirit controls an organization or a church or a life, He glorifies and exalts Jesus as Lord. In verse 15, Jesus includes a final reminder of the Holy Spirit's ministry.

"All things that the Father has are Mine; therefore I said, that He takes of Mine, and will disclose it to you."

III. Meaning to the Saint

How does all this apply to you and me? The answer lies in the two realms where the Holy Spirit works: *through* us and *to* us. First, *in convicting the world, the Spirit desires to use channels.* The Lord prefers to use living instruments as object lessons of His truth. He mentioned this earlier, in chapter 15, referring to believers as branches through which the vine produces fruit (vv. 1–5) and, in chapter 13, referring to love as one of the fruits of the Spirit: " 'By this all men will know that you are My disciples' " (v. 35). Second, *in communicating the Word, the Spirit desires to see changes.* His ultimate desire is to bring us into conformity with Jesus Christ. But to stamp that image on us requires change—change in what we acknowledge as truth and change in whom we glorify.

Let the Spirit Transform Your Life

In the mountains above the Los Angeles basin, towering transmission systems feed electricity to Southern California. Hundreds of thousands of electrical volts stream down to that basin. But who can use a hundred thousand volts in their home?

To parcel out this electricity into usable amounts, a system of transformers breaks down the voltage to 110- and 220-volt units. This allows the residents to plug into a virtually limitless power supply.

That's why it was necessary for Jesus to leave—to make room for the Transformer. And the Transformer will make available to you all the limitless forces that lie in Jesus . . . in quantities you can handle . . . in just the right amount for each situation.

If you're a Christian, you have access to that power. But unless you plug into it, you'll be running your life on your own effort, your own sweat, your own steam. That's like mashing potatoes by hand when you've got an electric mixer sitting on the counter beside you, or drying your hair with a towel when the blow dryer's within reach.

Is that how you want to live your Christian life?

Living Insights

More than anything else, the disciples needed to know that Jesus would not leave them on their own. The promise of the Holy Spirit was significant to them—as it is to us today.

● Carefully review John 16:4–15 and choose a dozen words that you consider key to understanding the Holy Spirit's ministry. Then consult a Bible dictionary to uncover a practical definition of each term. Finish up by writing out the definitions so you will remember them.

John 16:4–15

Verse _____ Key Word _____

Definition _____

Verse _____ Key Word _____

Definition _____

Verse _____ Key Word _____

Definition _____

Verse _____ Key Word _____

Definition _____

Verse _____ Key Word _____

Definition _____

Verse _____ Key Word _____

Definition _____

Verse _____ Key Word _____

Definition _____

Verse _____ Key Word _____

Definition _____

Verse _____ Key Word _____

Definition _____

Continued on next page

Verse _____ Key Word _____

Definition _____

Verse _____ Key Word _____

Definition _____

Verse _____ Key Word _____

Definition _____

 ## *Living Insights*

Study Two ▬▬▬▬▬▬▬▬▬▬▬▬▬▬▬▬▬▬▬▬▬▬▬

Toward the end of our lesson, we included two desires of the Holy Spirit. We could easily pass right over them without taking any time for application. But they are important. Let's take another look.

● The two desires of the Holy Spirit are restated below, with room to write in your response to each one.

1. In convicting the world, the Spirit desires to use *channels*. How are you being used as a channel?

_____

_____

_____

_____

2. In communicating the Word, the Spirit desires to see *changes*. How are you changing?

_____

_____

_____

_____

Four Words That Keep Us Going
John 16:16–33

The date: January 3, 1956
The place: Shell Mera, southeast of Quito, Ecuador
The hour: Early morning

Five men, whose names have become legend, sat quietly around a kitchen table praying in somber, whispered tones. Their prayers would prepare the way for face-to-face contact with the unreached, unpredictable Auca Indians deep in the interior of Ecuador. Their names: Jim Elliot, Pete Fleming, Nate Saint, Ed McCully, and Roger Youderian.

When the moment of departure arrived, the men began to sing a hymn they had come to love. Loudly and in unison the words rang out:

We rest on Thee, our Shield and our Defender,
Thine is the battle, Thine shall be the praise
When passing through the gates of pearly splendor
Victors, we rest with Thee through endless days.[1]

Minutes later, they were airborne. Days later, all five were dead, their lifeless bodies found floating on the Curaray River in Auca territory.

These brave missionaries left behind a legacy. They also left behind five widows, which begs the question: Who were the heroes—those who went, or those who stayed?

Staying is often more difficult than going. No doubt, the words of the hymn "We Rest on Thee, Our Shield" kept coming back to those wives as they suffered through the aftermath of that tragedy.

More than nineteen centuries earlier, another group sat around a table, this time set for twelve. One was destined for death. His name, too, has become legend: Jesus of Nazareth. We are told that when it was time to leave the room, those men sang a hymn as well.

One man—John—recorded what was spoken around the table that night. In the sixteenth chapter of his Gospel, we find Jesus' closing words to His men, who were bracing themselves to face life without the one they loved.

I. Confusion of the Disciples

Consternation quelled the appetites of the disciples; confusion crowded their minds, as verses 16–18 indicate.

"A little while, and you will no longer behold Me; and again a little while, and you will see Me." Some of His

---

1. "We Rest on Thee, Our Shield," by Edith Gilling Cherry.

disciples therefore said to one another, "What is this thing He is telling us, 'A little while, and you will not behold Me; and again a little while, and you will see Me'; and, 'because I go to the Father'?" And so they were saying, "What is this that He says, 'A little while'? We do not know what He is talking about."

Christ's main desire was to give the disciples hope, to lift their eyes from the tragedy of His departure to the glory of it. In doing so, He clarifies four major issues.

II. Clarification of the Issues

In his classic book *The Seven Laws of Teaching,* John Gregory states the Law of the Lesson: *"The truth to be taught must be learned through truth already known."*[2] Centuries before Gregory discovered this principle, Jesus used it to instruct His disciples, starting with the known and then taking them into the uncharted waters of the unknown. In verses 19–33, He summarizes the major issues and gives them four words on which to hang their hopes.

A. The issue of sorrow: *joy.* In the upper room, Jesus has mentioned impending sorrow and inevitable persecution several times. Now He wants to clarify that this isn't the end of their relationship.

> Jesus knew that they wished to question Him, and He said to them, "Are you deliberating together about this, that I said 'A little while, and you will not behold Me, and again a little while, and you will see Me'? Truly, truly, I say to you, that you will weep and lament, but the world will rejoice; you will be sorrowful, but your sorrow will be turned to joy." (vv. 19–20)

The disciples would go through incredible pain and sorrow, but their grief would not last forever. To illustrate this, Jesus draws a homespun analogy.

> "Whenever a woman is in travail she has sorrow, because her hour has come; but when she gives birth to the child, she remembers the anguish no more, for joy that a child has been born into the world." (v. 21)

No matter how intense the labor, once that tiny, priceless life is laid in your arms, the pain is forgotten. The comparison is clear.

> "Therefore you too now have sorrow; but I will see you again, and your heart will rejoice, and no one takes your joy away from you." (v. 22)

2. John Milton Gregory, *The Seven Laws of Teaching,* rev. ed. (1917; reprint, Grand Rapids, Mich.: Baker Book House, 1954), p. 68.

Just as a violent thunderstorm turns the desert into a bed of wildflowers, so the sorrowful storm to pass over the disciples would bloom joy in abundance. But this flower has deeper roots, as unearthed in verses 23–24.

> "And in that day you will ask Me no question. Truly, truly, I say to you, if you shall ask the Father for anything, He will give it to you in My name. Until now you have asked for nothing in My name; ask, and you will receive, that your joy may be made full."

The joy promised is not an ephemeral flower—here today, gone tomorrow. It's permanent and complete—a fully blossomed flower.

A Soothing Psalm for a Heavy Heart

Weeping may last for the night,
But a shout of joy comes in the morning.
(Ps. 30:5b)

B. The issue of access: *love*. Having broached the subject of prayer, Jesus clarifies the issue of God's accessibility.

> "These things I have spoken to you in figurative language; an hour is coming when I will speak no more to you in figurative language, but will tell you plainly of the Father. In that day you will ask in My name, and I do not say to you that I will request the Father on your behalf." (John 16:25–26)

There will come a time when the disciples will have direct access to the Father. And what will bring about this new relationship? Love.

> "For the Father Himself loves you, because you have loved Me, and have believed that I came forth from the Father." (v. 27)

In verse 28, Jesus puts His words well within the disciples' mental reach.

> "I came forth from the Father, and have come into the world; I am leaving the world again, and going to the Father."

And sure enough, the disciples get the picture.

> His disciples said, "Lo, now You are speaking plainly, and are not using a figure of speech." (v. 29)

Someone Up There Likes Me

Being assured of God's love does wonders to keep us going. No matter how rough the fight, His acceptance is

---

31

like spiritual adrenaline, supplying us with reserves of encouragement.

Do you find yourself in the ring, slugging it out with
life? Don't get discouraged. If God is in your corner, what
difference does it make how tough your opponent is?

If you're up against life's ropes right now, take a break
and towel off with these verses from Romans 8.

> Who shall separate us from the love of Christ?
> Shall tribulation, or distress, or persecution, or
> famine, or nakedness, or peril, or sword?...But
> in all these things we overwhelmingly conquer
> through Him who loved us. For I am convinced
> that neither death, nor life, nor angels, nor prin-
> cipalities, nor things present, nor things to come,
> nor powers, nor height, nor depth, nor any other
> created thing, shall be able to separate us from
> the love of God, which is in Christ Jesus our
> Lord. (vv. 35, 37–39)

Now get back in there—and keep punching!

C. The issue of knowledge: *faith.* Partial knowledge charac-
terized the disciples' lives. They grasped only a small portion
of what Jesus revealed to them. However, now more than ever,
their reach of faith needed to exceed what they could grasp.

> "Now we know that You know all things, and have no
> need for anyone to question You; by this we believe
> that You came from God." Jesus answered them, "Do
> you now believe?" (John 16:30–31)

Our faith in the Lord directly influences our growth in knowledge. The two are connected throughout Scripture. The Christian life starts with belief, and growth in Him continues in the
same way: "As you therefore have received Christ Jesus the Lord,
so walk in Him" (Col. 2:6). How did you receive Him? By faith.
How are you to walk in Him? By faith. And, if you look closely
at verse 30 of John 16—" 'we know that You know all things' " and
" 'we believe that You came from God' "—you see a clear statement of faith even in their confusion. In the days ahead, the
disciples' knowledge would come together; one by one, the
pieces would begin to fall into place, and the puzzle would become clear. And what made the puzzle clear were eyes of faith—
faith that the Lord not only knew all, but knew best. How about
you? Do you share the disciples' faith? When you trust that the
Lord knows best, your unanswered questions will be quieted.

D. The issue of separation: *peace*. If you do believe, your faith will be put to the test (James 1:2–4). For the disciples, their test was foretold in John 16:32.

"Behold, an hour is coming, and has already come,
for you to be scattered, each to his own home, and
to leave Me alone; and yet I am not alone, because
the Father is with Me."

But in the midst of that oncoming storm, there would be a calm.

"These things I have spoken to you, that in Me you
may have peace. In the world you have tribulation,
but take courage; I have overcome the world." (v. 33)

The source of their peace was not "in the world," but "in Me"; the strength of their courage was in the fact that "I have overcome the world."

III. Culmination of the Message

If we could put ourselves in the disciples' sandals, we probably would have walked very slowly toward Gethsemane that midnight hour. Our thoughts would naturally have sorted themselves into two overall impressions, probably much like the thoughts that went through the minds of those five missionary wives: Elisabeth Elliot . . . Olive Fleming . . . Marj Saint . . . Marilou McCully . . . Barbara Youderian. First and foremost would be this: *His life may not be long, but His death is no mistake.* Following on the heels of that thought would be another: *My life may not be easy, but I can go on if accompanied by joy, love, faith, and peace.*

A Song to Light Our Way

Christ is no longer on the earth in bodily form but lives in our hearts when we accept Him as Savior. He gives us joy, love, faith, and peace—and that's what keeps us going day by day.

Day by day and with each passing moment,
Strength I find to meet my trials here;
Trusting in my Father's wise bestowment,
I've no cause for worry or for fear.

He whose heart is kind beyond all measure
Gives unto each day what He deems best—
Lovingly, its part of pain and pleasure,
Mingling toil with peace and rest.[3]

Continued on next page

3. "Day by Day," by Lina Sandell.

🌳 *Living Insights*

Joy, love, faith, and peace—simple words, yet deeply significant for the Christian. They keep us going. These words are sprinkled throughout the Scriptures; let's look for them.

- With the help of a concordance, conduct a Scripture search. Look up these four words and find the corresponding passages in your Bible. In the chart that follows, list the verses and record a summary statement about each. If your time is limited, you could choose to research one word thoroughly or do a brief overview of all four words.

Joy, Love, Faith, Peace	
Verses	Summary Statements

◈ *Living Insights*

What keeps you going? This lesson demonstrated how four words help us. Do you tap into their enduring power? If not, why? If so, how have they helped you?

1. How has *joy* kept you going? _____

_____

_____

_____

2. How has *love* kept you going? _____

_____

_____

_____

3. How has *faith* kept you going? _____

_____

_____

_____

4. How has *peace* kept you going? _____

_____

_____

_____

5. What else keeps you going? _____

_____

_____

_____

Divine Intercession
John 17:1–19

Church historians credit the Reformation primarily to three men: Martin Luther, John Calvin, and John Knox. Luther is known for the commencement of the Reformation; Calvin, for its consummation; and Knox, for its preservation. Luther was the Reformation's torch; Calvin, its pen; Knox, its sword.

John Knox was indeed the sharp instrument of Scotland's Reformation. He wielded his carefully honed words widely and impartially, cutting a swath that touched even the royal robes of Mary, Queen of Scots.

Unaffectionately dubbed "Bloody Mary" because she sent some 290 evangelical church leaders to their deaths, this ruthless monarch opposed Knox with a passion. She banished the fiery luminary from his pulpit, but she could never extinguish his flaming influence. By the time he died, the Scottish Reformation was complete. Of that triumph, one historian noted:

> "It was the victory of the people, under the leadership of a brave
> and true man, against the combined forces of a queen, a court,
> and a powerful nobility. The Scotch reformers did their work so
> thoroughly that it was never necessary to do it over. They had
> written their protest with their own blood, and it stands to this
> day."[1]

But Knox was not only powerful in the pulpit; he was equally fervent on his knees. The Queen once commented that she feared the prayers of Knox as much as the combined armies of Scotland.

Though not as well known as his rugged intensity, there was also a tender side to Knox. As he lay dying, he whispered to his wife to read from the passage where he had cast his first anchor of faith—the seventeenth chapter of the Gospel of John.

Melanchthon, another reformer, said of this chapter shortly before his death:

> "There is no voice which has ever been heard, either in heaven
> or in earth, more exalted, more holy, more fruitful, more sublime,
> than the prayer offered up by the Son to God Himself."[2]

So, without further delay, get ready to cast your anchor into the deep but calm harbor of John 17.

---

1. As quoted by Elgin S. Moyer, *Great Leaders of the Christian Church* (Chicago, Ill.: Moody Press, 1951), p. 349.

2. As quoted by Arthur W. Pink, *Exposition of the Gospel of John,* vol. 1 (Grand Rapids, Mich.: Zondervan Publishing House, 1968), p. 90.

I. Historical and Geographical Setting

In this chapter we see the longest recorded prayer of Jesus—a prayer that more than any other should be labeled the Lord's Prayer.

A. The time. The Last Supper was over. It was late, probably past midnight, when Jesus and the disciples left that upper room and began making their way to Gethsemane.

B. The place. Comparing John 17:1 with 18:1 gives us some idea of the setting. En route to the garden of Gethsemane lay the Kidron ravine, a mute portent of Christ's death. A channel led from Jerusalem's temple altar to the ravine, collecting the blood of the 256,000 lambs slaughtered and sacrificed during that Passover. When Jesus crossed it, the ravine was doubtless red with blood. This was where He offered His prayer.

C. The occasion. With the smell of lambs' blood hanging heavy in the night air, Jesus knew His hour had come (see 18:4). But before that hour overtook Him, He took a momentary death-row reprieve to pray to the Father.

II. An Examination of the Prayer

Before we analyze its individual parts, let's stand back to get an overall perspective on the prayer.

A. An overview of the whole. In reading through these twenty-six verses, it's clear that three things were on the Lord's heart that night: Himself (17:1–5), His disciples (vv. 6–19), and the Church (vv. 20–26).

> These three sections are like three concentric circles, the second of which is larger than the first, and the third of which is larger than the second, and inclusive of all three. All, however, have a common center. The prayer as a whole is keyed to one central idea, *eternal life;* for it is Jesus' petition that He may be glorified in order that eternal life may be made available to men.[3]

We'll examine the first two circles in this lesson and cover the third in the following.

B. Analysis of the parts. The first circle drawn encloses only Christ.

　　1. Jesus praying for Himself. With His men close at hand, Jesus stops to focus His attention on the Father.

> These things Jesus spoke; and lifting up His eyes to heaven, He said, "Father, the hour has come; glorify Thy Son, that the Son may glorify Thee." (v. 1)

---

3. Merrill C. Tenney, *John: The Gospel of Belief* (Grand Rapids, Mich.: William B. Eerdmans Publishing Co., 1948), p. 244.

Six times in this prayer Jesus tenderly addresses God as "Father." His words dripping with emotion, Jesus speaks of His impending fate in the perfect tense, intoned with an air of finality: " 'the hour has come.' " But His death was no accidental tragedy. It was planned in the throne room of heaven, all the way down to the Judas kiss (Luke 22:22). In keeping with that plan, Jesus asks that He be exalted by His death, that it would shine like a beacon throughout all eternity, and that His God-given authority over men's souls might move from the realm of promise to the realm of fulfillment.

"Even as Thou gavest Him authority over all mankind, that to all whom Thou hast given Him, He may give eternal life. And this is eternal life, that they may know Thee, the only true God, and Jesus Christ whom Thou hast sent." (vv. 2–3)

Looking back on His life, Jesus reflects upon His relationship with the Father. On the basis of His past obedience, Jesus now turns His eyes to the future and requests that the glory He gave to the Father be reciprocated.

"I glorified Thee on the earth, having accomplished the work which Thou hast given Me to do. And now, glorify Thou Me together with Thyself, Father, with the glory which I had with Thee before the world was." (vv. 4–5)

When Jesus stepped down from His throne and became a man, He not only relinquished His crown, He gave up the glory He shared with the Father (compare Phil. 2:5–8). Now, as He prepares to return to the throne, Jesus asks for His old robe back—the regal garment of glory. This request the Father was delighted to fulfill (see Ps. 110, Eph. 1:20–23, Phil. 2:9–11).

2. **Jesus praying for His men.** Drawing another circle to include His most intimate friends, Jesus asks several things for these eleven men.

"I manifested Thy name to the men whom Thou gavest Me out of the world; Thine they were, and Thou gavest them to Me, and they have kept Thy word." (v. 6)

Manifest means "to reveal." During His three years with the disciples, Jesus revealed God's "name"—that is, His character and His resources. Jesus' response to disappointment, the serenity of His soul, the calm and quiet trust in His Father's will... all these qualities displayed the Father's name. The words that follow indicate that the Father truly had been made paramount in the minds of the disciples.

"Now they have come to know that everything Thou hast given Me is from Thee; for the words which Thou gavest Me I have given to them; and they received them, and truly understood that I came forth from Thee, and they believed that Thou didst send Me. I ask on their behalf; I do not ask on behalf of the world, but of those whom Thou hast given Me; for they are Thine; and all things that are Mine are Thine, and Thine are Mine; and I have been glorified in them." (vv. 7–10)

The Father's Word, they had kept (v. 6); His provisions, they had acknowledged (v. 7); His plan, they had accepted (v. 8); His glory, they had helped contribute to (vv. 9–10). Before the Good Shepherd lays down His life for His sheep, He prays that this intimate fold—certainly to be scared in His absence—may not be scattered.

"And I am no more in the world; and yet they themselves are in the world, and I come to Thee. Holy Father, keep them in Thy name, the name which Thou hast given Me, that they may be one, even as We are. While I was with them, I was keeping them in Thy name which Thou hast given Me; and I guarded them, and not one of them perished but the son of perdition, that the Scripture might be fulfilled. But now I come to Thee; and these things I speak in the world, that they may have My joy made full in themselves." (vv. 11–13)

With a flock as diverse as this one, unity was no small request. These were tough-minded, independent, strong-willed men. Matthew—a tax-law major and accounting minor. Peter—impulsive, impertinent, and at times, impetuous. James and John—brothers who were known as the "Sons of Thunder." The character and charisma of Jesus held these disparate, sometimes volatile, elements in a state of equilibrium. But He was about to be removed from the equation and feared this would cause the breakup of the bond between the men. Up to this point He had guarded them, but now He had to let them go.

Unity in Diversity

Jesus' overriding concern for His disciples was their unity, not their uniformity. He recognized their diversity. And He valued it.

39

Sometimes in our zeal to conform ourselves and others to the image of Christ, we forget that God doesn't xerox disciples. He uses our individuality to achieve a variety of purposes—to fight on different battlefields, to wage different wars, to wield different weapons. He uses His Luthers, Calvins, and Knoxes as torches, pens, and swords.

What's important is not that we're all swords but that we're all in the battle, fighting for the same King.

So, if the people around you aren't quite fitting the Sunday school mold—or even if they break the mold altogether—lighten up. God may be fashioning another Peter to turn the world upside down. Or another John Knox, for a reformation yet to come.

Jesus then asks the Father not only to keep the disciples together but to keep them from the enemy as well.

> "I have given them Thy word; and the world has
> hated them, because they are not of the world,
> even as I am not of the world. I do not ask Thee
> to take them out of the world, but to keep them
> from the evil one. They are not of the world, even
> as I am not of the world." (vv. 14–16)

Jesus' request in verse 15 logically follows. The enemy is always at work, so there's all the more reason to be unified. If the enemy can divide, he can conquer. There's also something in verse 15 that's easy to overlook, and that's what Jesus *didn't* ask. He didn't ask the Father to take them out of the world. He never intended them to retreat back into the saltshaker; He intended to have them sprinkled around! He never intended their lights to be put under a bushel; He intended for them to shine! True, we are not to be *of* the world. But we are to be *in* it. Philippians 2:15 strikes a good balance: you are to be "*above* reproach *in the midst* of a crooked and perverse generation, among whom you appear as lights in the world" (emphasis added). Earlier Christ prayed to "keep them" (v. 11); now He prays to "sanctify them."

> "Sanctify them in the truth; Thy word is truth."
> (v. 17)

The word *sanctify* is often misunderstood. It doesn't mean growing a halo or glowing with spirituality. It means "to set apart for a certain purpose or for an intended use." If you take food out of the refrigerator for dinner, in the biblical sense you have "sanctified" that food—set it apart for a

40

specific use. How are we to be sanctified? By the truth. And why are we to be sanctified? To become useful.

> "As Thou didst send Me into the world, I also have sent them into the world. And for their sakes I sanctify Myself, that they themselves also may be sanctified in truth." (vv. 18–19)

We become useful when the truth becomes such an integral part of us that it makes our lives distinctive. " 'You shall know the truth, and the truth shall make you free' " (8:32).

┌─ *Defeat by Default* ──────────────

If His Word is not working in us in a life-changing way, the world *will* be. If we are not becoming conformed to the image of Christ, we will be squeezed into the mold of the world (Rom. 12:2). Make no mistake about it: dusty Bibles lead to dirty lives.

III. How Does Christ's Prayer Relate to Us Today?

Remember John Knox? He said that he anchored his life in John 17. It was here he found strength. It was here he found stability. Why? What is here that isn't elsewhere? Two principles which applied to him, and apply to us as well.

A. Genuine accomplishment is determined by God, not man. In verse 4, Jesus speaks of having glorified God by already accomplishing the work that was given Him. But He was only thirty-three. He only reached eleven men in depth. Wasn't His life a tragic waste by being cut so short? Only when seen from a limited perspective! Man focuses on immediate results; God, on ultimate results. We see only the seed that is sown or, at best, the sprout; He sees the harvest.

B. Godly reinforcement is provided from heaven, not the world. In verses 9 and 11, Jesus appeals to the Father for unity, preservation, sanctification, and usefulness. These things don't come naturally to us. They are provided supernaturally. And they are not obtained through committee or by consensus. They are found only in Christ.

Continued on next page

Living Insights

Study One ▬▬▬▬▬▬▬▬▬▬▬▬▬▬▬▬▬▬▬▬▬▬▬▬▬▬▬▬

The seventeenth chapter of John's Gospel is certainly a moving scene in the life of Christ. His prayer is one of tender emotion and true sincerity. Some of you have spent time in this passage before; for others, it is brand new. Let's delve further into its depths by examining it in another version of Scripture.

- Read John 17 in a different version of the Scriptures. Often, it is through a fresh translation that certain truths strike us with even greater force. Try Phillip's paraphrase or the Living Bible, if you don't normally use them. Other translations are the New American Standard Bible, New International Version, New King James, King James, or Revised Standard Version.

Living Insights

Study Two ▬▬▬▬▬▬▬▬▬▬▬▬▬▬▬▬▬▬▬▬▬▬▬▬▬▬▬▬

Intercession makes us glad. To think that someone would pray on our behalf is encouragement in itself. Put on top of that Jesus' intercession for us and we have a mind-boggling thought! Let's use our time today to demonstrate Christlikeness. Let's practice intercessory prayer.

- Let's use this Living Insights as a time for prayer. But it is important to clarify one point: Today we pray for other people, not ourselves. Space is provided below to make a list of those you want to remember in prayer.

_____	_____
_____	_____
_____	_____
_____	_____
_____	

When Jesus Prayed for You

John 17:20–26

In his sweep toward world domination, Alexander the Great was marching to Jerusalem. The citizens of that city waited in terror, grimly aware of the might of Alexander's army and the trail of blood it splattered in its wake.

The Jewish historian Josephus recounted the details of that fearful moment when the Greeks met face-to-face with the Jews. Outside the walls of Zion stood Jaddua, the high priest, surrounded by many priests and citizens, all dressed in solid white robes. Jaddua wore a liturgical headdress bearing the name of God on a golden plate.

Unexpectedly, Alexander called his army to a halt and approached the high priest, intrigued not by the man's office but by the name he so prominently displayed. Puzzled, Alexander told the priest that he had dreamed this very scene.

From an old sheath, the priest drew out a well-worn scroll of Isaiah. He showed Alexander chapters 7 and 8 of Daniel's prophecy, written over two hundred years before. It was a prophecy which, in symbolic language, foretold that the Greeks would defeat the Persians and that their leader would become great.

Alexander was seeing his own reflection in that prophecy. In a moment of understanding and awe, he not only spared Jerusalem from being pillaged but treated the Jews there with dignity.

Just as Alexander saw himself in Daniel's prophecy, so we can see ourselves in Jesus' prayer in John 17. He doesn't call us by name, but it is clear that He had each of us in mind.

"I do not ask in behalf of these alone, but for those also who believe in Me through their word." (v. 20)

Like Alexander, we should be awed and overjoyed to know that the Scripture includes *us*. Let's take some time to eavesdrop on an ancient prayer in our behalf.

I. The Ministry of Prayer

Prayer is pivotal to the spiritual life, as spiritual men of the Bible inform us. Jesus instructed that "at all times they ought to pray and not to lose heart" (Luke 18:1). The apostle Paul emphasized the priority of prayer: "First of all, then, I urge that ... prayers ... be made" (1 Tim. 2:1). James, the practical exhorter of the New Testament, added: "You do not have because you do not ask" (James 4:2b). Samuel, the godly judge of Israel, declared: "Far be it from me that I

43

should sin against the Lord by ceasing to pray for you" (1 Sam. 12:23). In his command to put on the whole armor of God, Paul instructed the Ephesians to "pray at all times in the Spirit" (Eph. 6:18).

II. The Prayer of Jesus

Let's review John 17 before we examine verses 20–26 in detail.

A. Review. In verses 1–5, Jesus prays for Himself. In verses 6–19, He prays for the eleven remaining disciples. Finally, in verses 20–26, the Lord prays for all future believers.

B. Intercession. Three specific matters were on Jesus' heart regarding all His followers.

1. **He prayed for our unity.** In verses 21–23, notice the three similar phrases Jesus uses to make His point:

> "*That they may all be one;* even as Thou, Father, art in Me, and I in Thee, that they also may be in Us; that the world may believe that Thou didst send Me. And the glory which Thou hast given Me I have given to them; *that they may be one,* just as We are one; I in them, and Thou in Me, *that they may be perfected in unity,* that the world may know that Thou didst send Me, and didst love them, even as Thou didst love Me." (emphasis added)

First, Jesus prays for *unity of belief* (vv. 20b–21a). This unity originates from shared convictions. In the narthex of an impressive church in Berkeley, California, hang huge portraits of influential human leaders: Ghandi, Lincoln, Jesus, Luther, a president, a philosopher. Engraved in bronze above them is a quotation from the Bible. It reads, "Ye are all the children of God." The quote is from Galatians 3:26. But the last part of the verse is omitted—"by faith in Christ Jesus" (KJV). Belief is what binds us together. Not a vague, nebulous faith, but a very specific faith in Jesus Christ. The second thing Jesus prays for is *unity in glory* (v. 22). What does this mean? In verses 6 and 8, Jesus spoke of giving His followers two specific things: His name and His Word; that is, resources and direction. We are united because we draw from the same resources and follow the same directions. And that is what brings glory to God. If you read the passage closely, you'll discover a major purpose for this unity: that the world may *believe* that God sent Christ (v. 21) and that they may *know* this and that He loved them as He loved His Son (v. 23). Our unity is a public witness, an announcement to the world that Jesus came from God and that God's love rests upon us as on His own Son.

That They May Be One

When Jesus prays, it's not for uniformity—absolute similarity of organization, style, personality, and appearance. Neither does He pray for unanimity—absolute agreement of opinion within a group of people. Nor does He pray for union—absolute coalition or tight affiliation within the ranks of Christianity. What He does pray for is unity—oneness of heart, of faith, and of purpose.

> Within the church of historic Christianity there have been wide divergences of opinion and ritual. Unity, however, prevails wherever there is a deep and genuine experience of Christ; for the fellowship of the new birth transcends all historical and denominational boundaries. Paul of Tarsus, Luther of Germany, Wesley of England, and Moody of America would find deep unity with each other, though they were widely separated by time, by space, by nationality, by educational background, and by ecclesiastical connections.[1]

Jesus doesn't pray for uniformity of practice or unanimity of thinking or union between all religious organizations. What He does pray for is unity . . . a oneness which only the Holy Spirit can bring about. And that can't be achieved through committee or consensus. Only through faith in, and love for, Jesus.

2. He prayed for our destiny. In verse 24, Jesus prays: "Father, I desire that they also, whom Thou hast given Me, be with Me where I am, in order that they may behold My glory, which Thou hast given Me; for Thou didst love Me before the foundation of the world."

In this prayer, our Lord asks the Father to secure our destiny. That security is based on the love between the Father and the Son. Can you imagine a foundation more secure? His prayer was that we be with Him in heaven, where He would be surrounded in glory.

1. Merrill C. Tenney, *John: The Gospel of Belief* (Grand Rapids, Mich.: William B. Eerdmans Publishing Co., 1948), p. 249.

The promise of glory is the promise, almost incredible and only possible by the work of Christ,
that some of us, that any of us who really
chooses, . . . shall find approval, shall please God.
To please God . . . to be a real ingredient in the
divine happiness . . . to be loved by God, not
merely pitied, but delighted in as an artist de-
lights in his work or a father in a son—it seems
impossible, a weight or burden of glory which
our thoughts can hardly sustain. But so it is.[2]

3. **He prayed for relational love.** Observe carefully as Jesus
calls to mind that perfect relationship between Himself and
the Father.

"O righteous Father, although the world has not
known Thee, yet I have known Thee; and these
have known that Thou didst send Me; and I have
made Thy name known to them, and will make it
known; that the love wherewith Thou didst love
Me may be in them, and I in them." (vv. 25–26)

The Father loves the Son, the Son loves us, and we, in turn,
are to love others. This love flows deep and wide and passes
over any rocks of petty differences.

III. The Application of the Message

Three specific applications emerge from verses 20–26.

A. **To grow in unity means *giving in*.** It means refusing to
get hung up on trivial disagreements or particular philosophies.
Those who enjoy Christian fellowship in its deepest sense have
high tolerance levels.

B. **To know your destiny means *giving up*.** Being secure in
our future requires that we stop striving and simply give up and
trust Him.

C. **To show His love means *giving out*.** Christian love is visible and tangible. God not only tells us He loves us, He shows it.

But God demonstrates His own love toward us, in
that while we were yet sinners, Christ died for us.
(Rom. 5:8)

The Demise of Alexander the Great

The death of Alexander was as tragic as his life was remarkable. He died at thirty-three, an alcoholic with no
more worlds to conquer.

---

2. C. S. Lewis, *The Weight of Glory and Other Addresses* (Grand Rapids, Mich.: William B.
Eerdmans Publishing Co., 1965), p. 10.

He had a flash of understanding when he caught a glimpse of himself in Scripture. But the glory of personal triumph outshone the glory of God in his eyes, and his moment of clear thinking never blossomed into a lifetime of Christian commitment.

> But prove yourselves doers of the word, and
> not merely hearers who delude themselves. For
> if anyone is a hearer of the word and not a doer,
> he is like a man who looks at his natural face
> in a mirror; for once he has looked at himself
> and gone away, he has immediately forgotten
> what kind of person he was. (James 1:22–24)

Don't be an Alexander who takes only a passing glance into the mirror of Scripture. Look diligently into God's Word and allow it to change you.

> But one who looks intently at the perfect law,
> the law of liberty, and abides by it, not having
> become a forgetful hearer but an effectual doer,
> this man shall be blessed in what he does. (v. 25)

🐫 *Living Insights*

Study One ▬▬▬▬▬▬▬▬▬▬▬▬▬▬▬▬▬▬▬▬▬▬▬▬▬▬▬▬

Prayer has at least five specific categories for us to remember and employ: confession, praise, thanksgiving, intercession, and petition. Let's find out what the Bible says about each one.

- Look up the following verses that relate to each category of prayer and use the accompanying charts to record your observations.

Confession: Admitting your sin and asking for forgiveness on the merit of Christ's blood at the cross

References	Observations
Ps. 32:5	
Ps. 51:1–4	
1 John 1:9	

Continued on next page

Praise: Expressing worship and adoration to the Godhead

References	Observations
1 Chron. 29:10–12	
Ps. 150	
Rev. 4:10–11	

Thanksgiving: Acknowledging, with gratitude, God's provision for us

References	Observations
Ps. 103:1–8	
Eph. 5:20	
1 Thess. 5:18	

Intercession: Upholding others who are in need

References	Observations
1 Sam. 12:23	
Acts 12:5	
1 Tim. 2:1–2	

Petition: Representing our own needs and requests

References	Observations
Matt. 7:7–8	
Heb. 4:14–16	
James 1:5–8	

 Living Insights

If you're a Christian, Jesus prayed His intercessory prayer for you. He asked for spiritual unity, eternal destiny, and relational love. From these requests, we can derive three applications, listed below.

• Jot down some practical ways you can demonstrate each of the following principles over the next few weeks. Think carefully. Be realistic. And do them.

To grow in unity means *giving in.*

1. _____
2. _____
3. _____

To know your destiny means *giving up.*

1. _____
2. _____
3. _____

To show His love means *giving out.*

1. _____
2. _____
3. _____

Arrest and Trial
John 18:1–24

For three and a half years, Jesus had been watched by an official band of Jewish religious leaders whose hostility grew with each passing month. With the cunning of foxes and the ruthlessness of wolves, this unholy alliance plotted Jesus' demise.

The final scenes were staged with meticulous care. An insider was contracted to help orchestrate the arrest—Judas. And with a mere thirty pieces of silver—the going price for a slave—the betrayal was sealed. At an earlier appointed time, Judas notified the officials of Jesus' whereabouts, accompanied them to the site, identified the accused with a kiss, and then got out of the way. The soldiers did the rest.

As we pick up the story in John 18, the plot has reached its climax. It is late at night; Jesus has just finished praying in the garden of Gethsemane. It's a vulnerable, private spot, away from the city buildings that might hide Him and the crowds who might protect Him.

> But the privacy of the Passion story ended at this moment. A clanking of men and arms was starting to shatter the hush of night. Quivering daggers of orange flame began stabbing the horizon to the west, and soon a procession of torches filed into the grove.[1]

What irony. With lanterns and torches, the Roman cohort[2] searches to find the Light of the World (John 18:1–3). And the Light just stands there—without pretense, without protection—and shines openly through the darkness. But those standing in the darkness do not even recognize Him (1:5).

I. The Arrest
The whole garden is awash with light that spills from the lanterns and torches, revealing twelve suspicious-looking men, their shadows long and gaunt in the torchlight. Instinctively, the soldiers clutch the hilts of their swords. But they are disarmed by a soft-spoken question.

> Jesus therefore, knowing all the things that were coming upon Him, went forth, and said to them, "Whom do you seek?" They answered Him, "Jesus the Nazarene." He said to them, "I am He." And Judas also who was betraying

---

1. Paul L. Maier, *First Easter* (New York, N.Y.: Harper and Row, Publishers, 1973), p. 39.

2. The Greek word is *speira*. A cohort was the tenth part of a legion and normally comprised 600 men (though this number varied from 200 to 1,200). It was commanded by a *chiliarchos* (see v. 12). The large number of soldiers not only ensured the success of the arrest but also would have been able to stave off any riot that might ensue.

Him, was standing with them. When therefore He said to them, "I am He," they drew back, and fell to the ground. Again therefore He asked them, "Whom do you seek?" And they said, "Jesus the Nazarene." Jesus answered, "I told you that I am He; if therefore you seek Me, let these go their way," that the word might be fulfilled which He spoke, "Of those whom Thou hast given Me I lost not one." (18:4–9)

Like a lamb, silent before its shearers, Jesus offers no resistance (Isa. 53:7). Not so with Peter. Instead, he does a little shearing of his own.

Simon Peter therefore having a sword, drew it, and struck the high priest's slave, and cut off his right ear; and the slave's name was Malchus. (John 18:10)

Jesus responds resolutely.

"Put the sword into the sheath; the cup which the Father has given Me, shall I not drink it?" (v. 11)

The snare is tripped; the prey is caught. Mission accomplished.

So the Roman cohort and the commander, and the officers of the Jews, arrested Jesus and bound Him. (v. 12)

The text states the event matter-of-factly. But the reality behind those words was brutal.

The proper manner, taught by the academy of soldiery in Rome, was to take the victim by the right wrist, twist his arm behind him so that his knuckles touched between his shoulder blades and, at the same time, jam the heel down on his right instep. This was the beginning of the pain Jesus would feel this day.[3]

Three things stand out in this arrest. First, Jesus had not slept that night. But even though He is fatigued, He never loses control. Second, He responds willingly. He doesn't resist, and His captors are totally unprepared for this (see v. 6). In other circumstances, they had been unable to seize Him (see 7:30, 44; 10:39). But now His hour has come, and He willingly gives Himself up. The final thing we notice in the passage is His compassion, both for the disciples (18:8–9) and for the soldiers (vv. 10–11). There would be no blood shed besides His. Jesus made sure of that. Even the slave's wounded ear is healed (Luke 22:51).

II. The Trials

From this point on, Jesus is no longer free. He becomes the property of the state, railroaded through the most fallacious, unfair, disorderly,

---

3. Jim Bishop, *The Day Christ Died* (New York, N.Y.: Harper and Row, Publishers, 1965), pp. 196–97.

illegal series of trials in the history of jurisprudence. No man was ever more innocent. No trials were ever more unjust.

A. A survey. In all, there are six trials—three Jewish, three Roman (the chart accompanying this lesson briefly summarizes the trials). The charge in the Jewish trials is blasphemy; in the Roman trials, it is treason. Since the Jews are not allowed to administer capital punishment, they turn to the Roman authorities, which explains why Jesus is crucified instead of stoned.

B. Jewish regulations. The Jews took their legal instructions from the Mosaic Law as interpreted for them in the Talmud. Judged according to this scale, the trials are weighed and found wanting.

1. **Arrest** for a capital crime must be made in broad daylight, not at night. Verdict: law ignored.

2. **Arrest** for a capital crime may not be made based on information by the offender's follower—for if the accused were a criminal, so were his followers. Verdict: law ignored.

3. **No Jewish** trial may be held at night; that is, between 6 P.M. and 6 A.M. Furthermore, never is a trial to be held before only one person, so that partiality or prejudice can be avoided. Verdict: laws ignored. Two of the three trials occur some time between 2 and 6 A.M., and they are before single individuals.

4. **Members** of the Jewish court, after hearing testimony regarding the one accused of a capital crime, are not permitted to render an immediate verdict, but are required instead to return to their homes for two days and nights, eating only light food, drinking only light wines, and sleeping well. Then they are to return and hear again the testimony against the accused and cast their vote. Verdict: law ignored.

5. **The Sanhedrin** must vote one at a time, the younger men first, so as not to be influenced by the older men on the council. In the third trial, they all vote simultaneously. Verdict: law ignored. Conclusion: this entire set of Jewish trials is a gross miscarriage of procedural law.

C. Jewish trials. Under Jewish law, no one person could act as a judge. The verdict was decided by a "court" of at least three. A more important case might be judged by a band of twenty-three, known as the Lesser Sanhedrin. The ultimate court was the Greater Sanhedrin, consisting of seventy to seventy-three men.

1. **Before Annas.** Notice that Jesus is tried illegally during the hours of darkness, by one man—Annas. Annas, the father-in-law of Caiaphas the high priest, is comparable to a Mafia

52

boss. He is the wealthiest and most influential man of the city. He owns and operates the entire money-changing system, which is corrupt to the core and behind the group Jesus chased out of the temple. He has served as the high priest for seventeen years and is now the high priest emeritus. He is the power behind the throne in Jewry. And ever since Jesus upset his business in the temple courtyard, Annas has had a personal vendetta against Him. Gloating, the seventy-year-old Annas probes Jesus on two counts: His teaching and His disciples (John 18:19). Jesus' response in verses 20–21 seems impudent, but He is merely placing the legal burden of proof on Annas's shoulders where it rightfully belongs. A soldier rescues Annas from embarrassment by slapping Jesus down to size and putting Him in His place.

2. **Before Caiaphas.** Caiaphas is the current high priest, the weak son-in-law of Annas, a pawn of Rome, equally corrupt but probably not as clever as Annas (v. 24). To grasp the full impact of the trial, let's take a look at Mark 14.

And they led Jesus away to the high priest; and all the chief priests and the elders and the scribes gathered together. And Peter had followed Him at a distance, right into the courtyard of the high priest; and he was sitting with the officers, and warming himself at the fire. Now the chief priests and the whole Council kept trying to obtain testimony against Jesus to put Him to death; and they were not finding any. For many were giving false testimony against Him, and yet their testimony was not consistent. And some stood up and began to give false testimony against Him, saying, "We heard Him say, 'I will destroy this temple made with hands, and in three days I will build another made without hands.' " And not even in this respect was their testimony consistent. And the high priest stood up and came forward and questioned Jesus, saying, "Do You make no answer? What is it that these men are testifying against You?" But He kept silent, and made no answer. Again the high priest was questioning Him, and saying to Him, "Are You the Christ, the Son of the Blessed One?" And Jesus said, "I am; and you shall see the Son of Man sitting at the right hand of Power, and coming with the clouds of heaven." And tearing his clothes, the high priest said, "What further need do we have of witnesses? You have heard the blasphemy; how does it seem to you?" And they all condemned Him to be deserving of death. And some began to spit at Him, and to blindfold Him, and to beat Him with their fists, and to say to Him, "Prophesy!" And the officers received Him with slaps in the face. (vv. 53–65)

This is nothing more than a kangaroo court. It is illegal because it takes place during the night, because a "preliminary hearing" isn't allowed, and because they aren't in their chamber. Not to mention the deck of false witnesses stacked against Jesus (vv. 56–59). What brings everyone to their feet in outcry against the accused is our Lord's reply to Caiaphas's interrogation in verse 61. The high priest asks Him point-blank: "Are you the Messiah?" Jesus looks him square in the eye and answers: "I am" (v. 62). He elaborates with messianic quotes from Psalm 110:1 and Daniel 7:13, and that is the straw that breaks the court's back.

Coping with Undeserved Suffering

Jesus was slandered and treated inhumanly by a religious and legal system bent on His destruction. But where others would cry "Mistrial," He demanded no appeal.

Every step of His way to the cross, Jesus left behind an example of how to bear up under suffering unjustly imposed.

For this finds favor, if for the sake of conscience toward God a man bears up under sorrows when suffering unjustly. For what credit is there if, when you sin and are harshly treated, you endure it with patience? But if when you do what is right and suffer for it you patiently endure it, this finds favor with God. For you have been called for this purpose, since Christ also suffered for you, leaving you an example for you to follow in His steps, who committed no sin, nor was any deceit found in His mouth; and while being reviled, He did not revile in return; while suffering, He uttered no threats, but kept entrusting Himself to Him who judges righteously. (1 Pet. 2:19–23)

The key to Christ's attitude was trust—not in the legal system or the religious institutions but in "Him who judges righteously."

Are you going through trials and persecutions right now? Have friends betrayed or deserted you? Are your enemies having a field day with your reputation? Are they spreading lies about you?

If so, look to the Father. He sees. He knows. He judges righteously. Someday your case will be heard in heaven, and then you will be vindicated. As for now, take comfort in the fact that He cares and loves you and will not let this injustice go on forever!

Continued on next page

THE TRIALS OF JESUS CHRIST

Trial	Officiating Authority	Scripture	Accusation	Legality	Type	Result
1	Annas, ex-high priest of the Jews (A.D. 6–15).	John 18:13–23	Trumped-up charges of irreverence to Annas.	ILLEGAL! Held at night. No specific charges. Prejudice. Violence.	Jewish and Religious	Found guilty of irreverence and rushed to Caiaphas.
2	Caiaphas—Annas's son-in-law—and the Sanhedrin (A.D. 18–36).	Matthew 26:57–68 Mark 14:53–65 John 18:24	Claiming to be the Messiah, the Son of God . . . blasphemy (worthy of death under Jewish law).	ILLEGAL! Held at night. False witnesses. Prejudice. Violence.	Jewish and Religious	Declared guilty of blasphemy and rushed to the Sanhedrin (Jewish supreme court).
3	The Sanhedrin—seventy ruling men of Israel (their word was needed before He could be taken to Roman officials).	Mark 15:1a Luke 22:66–71	Claiming to be the Son of God . . . blasphemy.	ILLEGAL! Accusation switched. No witnesses. Improper voting.	Jewish and Religious	Declared guilty of blasphemy and rushed to Roman official, Pilate.
4	Pilate, governor of Judea, who was already in "hot water" with Rome (A.D. 26–36).	Matthew 27:11–14 Mark 15:1b–5 Luke 23:1–7 John 18:28–38	Treason (accusation was changed, since treason was worthy of capital punishment in Rome).	ILLEGAL! Christ was kept under arrest, although He was found innocent. No defense attorney. Violence.	Roman and Civil	Found innocent . . . but rushed to Herod Antipas; mob overruled Pilate.
5	Herod Antipas, governor of Galilee (4 B.C.–A.D. 39).	Luke 23:8–12	No accusation was made.	ILLEGAL! No grounds. Mockery in courtroom. No defense attorney. Violence.	Roman and Civil	Mistreated and mocked; returned to Pilate without decision made by Herod.
6	Pilate (second time).	Matthew 27:15–26 Mark 15:6–15 Luke 23:18–25 John 18:39–19:16	Treason, though not proven (Pilate bargained with the mob, putting Christ on a level with Barabbas, a criminal).	ILLEGAL! Without proof of guilt, Pilate allowed an innocent man to be condemned.	Roman and Civil	Found innocent, but Pilate "washed hands" and allowed Him to be crucified.

Living Insights

Study One ■■■■■■■■■■■■■■■■■■■■■■■■■■■■■■■■■■■■■

The four Gospels tell the story of Jesus, but from different perspectives. We have the benefit of reading several eyewitness accounts of the same historical events. And, like anyone, each writer focuses on different aspects, particular details, and specific conversations. As we come to the arrest and trials of Jesus, we find John's story enhanced by the viewpoints of Matthew, Mark, and Luke.

● In order to gain some added insight, let's take a look at the parallel accounts of Jesus' arrest and trials. You'll find these in Matthew 26–27, Mark 14–15, and Luke 22–23. When you've finished reading, summarize the events in the space provided for you.

Summary of the Arrest and Trials of Christ

_____

_____

_____

_____

_____

_____

_____

_____

_____

_____

_____

_____

_____

_____

_____

_____

_____

Continued on next page

Living Insights

Many a believer has found support and encouragement from the rich lyrics in the great hymns of our faith. How long has it been since you've taken a really good look at the words of those familiar songs?

- Locate a familiar hymnbook. As you page through it, look particularly for hymns relating to the sufferings of Christ. The arrest and trials were just the beginning of what He endured on our behalf. Allow these hymns to speak to your heart. Conclude your time by singing aloud one of your favorite hymns.

Rush to Judgment

John 18:28–19:16

Uniting against a common enemy often makes for an unusual alliance. The United States and Russia, for example, joined forces against Hitler in World War II.

Uncommon alliances also formed against Christ. One such partnership existed between the Pharisees and the Herodians.

> And the Pharisees went out and immediately began taking counsel with the Herodians against Him, as to how they might destroy Him. (Mark 3:6)

Yet these special-interest groups sat at opposite political poles.

> For while Herodians supported Rome, and everything Greek or Roman, excusing Herod's infamous immoralities, the Pharisees opposed all foreign influence and maintained a most rigorous puritanism. Yet [they] find common cause in putting Christ to death.[1]

In today's lesson, we see avowed enemies join hands to annihilate Jesus. First is the coupling of Pilate and Herod, bitter enemies.

> Herod's family had once ruled Palestine for the Romans and resented the appointment of procurators in Judea. Pilate had once at least invaded Galilee to suppress revolt, treading upon Herod's toes, and suspected that Herod sent secret reports to Caesar about Jewish affairs. Yet against Jesus they are united, and that fateful day become "friends". [see Luke 23:12][2]

A second unholy alliance forms between the Jews and Caesar.

> Add to these Caiaphas, declaring publicly to a Roman governor, amid Passover memories of ancient liberation, "We have no king but Caesar!" Caiaphas and Caesar, Israel and Rome—strange friendship indeed![3]

And so, in a rush to judgment, archenemies become sudden allies.

I. Christ before the Sanhedrin

The Sanhedrin was the supreme court of the Jews, with complete jurisdiction over all religious and theological matters. The members

1. Reginald E. O. White, *Beneath the Cross of Jesus: Meditations on the Passion of our Lord* (New Canaan, Conn.: Keats Publishing, 1975), p. 96.

2. White, *Beneath the Cross,* p. 96.

3. White, *Beneath the Cross,* p. 96.

met in a place called the "council chamber," located in the Hall of Hewn Stone in the temple (Luke 22:66). There, and only there, could they carry out official business. And then, according to the Talmud, it had to be done during daylight hours. Luke is careful to note that the verdict against Christ was arrived at "when it was day" (22:66; see also Mark 15:1). The Sanhedrin was punctilious in its protocol. The members sat in a semicircle so that they could see one another. All charges against an alleged criminal had to be supported by the evidence of two witnesses, independently examined. When the verdict was due, the vote was taken one by one, from the youngest to the oldest, so that the younger members would not be swayed by the votes of the older members. Also, for a case where the death penalty might be evoked, the verdict could not be given on the same day as the trial. The members had to go home and give thought to their decision before returning their verdict. With the possible exception of the seating arrangement, all these procedures were ignored when the Sanhedrin tried Christ. Luke 22:66–71 is a record of the "official" meeting. In this passage, you will find no witnesses, no proven evidence, and no proper courtroom procedure. In probably the shortest of the six trials, lasting no more than twenty to thirty minutes, you will find only one thing—a rush to judgment.

II. Christ before Pilate

Because, under Roman law, the Jews were prohibited from putting someone to death, they had to send Jesus to stand trial before the governor—Pilate. But this posed a problem. The Sanhedrin accused Jesus of blasphemy. But that wouldn't hold water in the Roman court of an empire that recognized no Supreme Being beyond Caesar. So the accusation was altered, to treason. The code of law was different too. No longer was the Talmud followed; the Roman code of criminal procedure was used instead. This code involves four major steps, and all are found in the scene where Christ is brought before Pilate.

A. Step one: accusation. In John 18:28–32, the Roman trial begins.

> They led Jesus therefore from Caiaphas into the Praetorium, and it was early; and they themselves did not enter into the Praetorium in order that they might not be defiled, but might eat the Passover. Pilate therefore went out to them, and said, "What accusation do you bring against this Man?" They answered and said to him, "If this Man were not an evildoer, we would not have delivered Him up to you." Pilate therefore said to them, "Take Him yourselves, and judge Him according to your law." The Jews said to him, "We are not permitted to put anyone to death," that

the word of Jesus might be fulfilled, which He spoke, signifying by what kind of death He was about to die.

B. Step two: interrogation. In verses 33–35, Pilate begins formal questioning, probing for evidence to see if Jesus is, in fact, involved in a covert plan to overthrow the state.

Pilate therefore entered again into the Praetorium, and summoned Jesus, and said to Him, "Are You the King of the Jews?" Jesus answered, "Are you saying this on your own initiative, or did others tell you about Me?" Pilate answered, "I am not a Jew, am I? Your own nation and the chief priests delivered You up to me; what have You done?"

C. Step three: defense. Up to this point, Jesus has been either silent or evasive. Now He is given the opportunity to defend Himself.

Jesus answered, "My kingdom is not of this world. If My kingdom were of this world, then My servants would be fighting, that I might not be delivered up to the Jews; but as it is, My kingdom is not of this realm." Pilate therefore said to Him, "So You are a king?" Jesus answered, "You say correctly that I am a king. For this I have been born, and for this I have come into the world, to bear witness to the truth. Everyone who is of the truth hears My voice." Pilate said to Him, "What is truth?" (vv. 36–38a)

D. Step four: verdict. Convinced that Jesus is not a threat to Rome and that His activities aren't treasonous, Pilate renders the verdict.

And when he had said this, he went out again to the Jews, and said to them, "I find no guilt in Him." (v. 38b)

III. Christ before Herod

Turning to Luke 23, we find that when Pilate announces his verdict, the onlooking religious rabble rises up in protest.

But they kept on insisting, saying, "He stirs up the people, teaching all over Judea, starting from Galilee, even as far as this place." (v. 5)

When Pilate hears the word *Galilee,* he suddenly realizes a way out of his dilemma.

Pilate ... asked whether the man was a Galilean. And when he learned that He belonged to Herod's jurisdiction, he sent Him to Herod, who himself also was in Jerusalem at that time. (vv. 6–7)

Herod Antipas, the vice-tetrarch of Galilee, has beheaded John the Baptist, the forerunner of Jesus (Matt. 14:1–12). Herod has heard rumors of Jesus but has never taken Him seriously, thinking of Him more as a carnival Christ, a religious side show.

> Now Herod was very glad when he saw Jesus; for he had wanted to see Him for a long time, because he had been hearing about Him and was hoping to see some sign performed by Him. And he questioned Him at some length; but He answered him nothing. And the chief priests and the scribes were standing there, accusing Him vehemently. And Herod with his soldiers, after treating Him with contempt and mocking Him, dressed Him in a gorgeous robe and sent Him back to Pilate. Now Herod and Pilate became friends with one another that very day; for before they had been at enmity with each other. (Luke 23:8–12)

In the face of raucous jesting and vulgar innuendos, Jesus stands in regal dignity, silent and composed. This infuriates His enemies, who wrap a kingly robe around Him in mockery and return Him to sender.

IV. Christ before Pilate

Again, a sharp rap on the door brings Pilate face-to-face with this enigmatic Jesus.

A. Playing upon sympathy. Worming out of any decisive action, Pilate walks the tightrope between upholding justice and placating the people.

> And Pilate summoned the chief priests and the rulers and the people, and said to them, "You brought this man to me as one who incites the people to rebellion, and behold, having examined Him before you, I have found no guilt in this man regarding the charges which you make against Him. No, nor has Herod, for he sent Him back to us; and behold, nothing deserving death has been done by Him. I will therefore punish Him and release Him." (vv. 13–16)

Pilate thinks he can rough Jesus up and then release Him. But the people say no!

B. Bargaining with Barabbas. When Pilate realizes he's up against a wall, he takes another route, which Matthew traces in chapter 27, verses 15–18.

> Now at the [Passover] feast the governor was accustomed to release for the multitude any one prisoner whom they wanted. And they were holding at that time a notorious prisoner, called Barabbas. When therefore they were gathered together, Pilate said to

them, "Whom do you want me to release for you?
Barabbas, or Jesus who is called Christ?" For he knew
that because of envy they had delivered Him up.

Pilate attempts to use a convicted criminal as a bargaining chip
with this hardened crowd. Barabbas is termed a "notorious"
prisoner. The Greek word—*episēmon*—means "bearing a mark";
in other words, he's a marked man, probably on the Ten Most
Wanted list. The name Barabbas comes from the compound
consisting of *bar,* meaning "son," and *abba,* meaning "father."
Since well-known rabbis were given the title "father," it's possible
that Barabbas was the rebel son of some established religious
authority. Matthew tells us that this Barabbas was held as a
prisoner; Mark tells us why.

And the man named Barabbas had been imprisoned
with the insurrectionists who had committed murder
in the insurrection. (15:7)

Pilate gambles that this crowd, which he finds impervious to
emotional appeal, will reason rationally in weighing the guilt of
Barabbas against that of Jesus. But Pilate loses. The chant "Give
us Barabbas!" echoes through the streets. So the murderer goes
free. Stymied, Pilate tries a last-ditch effort to release Jesus, but
again the crowd hems him in a corner.

As a result of this Pilate made efforts to release Him,
but the Jews cried out, saying, "If you release this
Man, you are no friend of Caesar; everyone who makes
himself out to be a king opposes Caesar." (John 19:12)

With these words, the crowd places on Pilate's back the political
straw that brings him to his knees.

When Pilate therefore heard these words, he brought
Jesus out, and sat down on the judgment seat at a place
called The Pavement, but in Hebrew, Gabbatha. (v. 13)

Matthew tells us that Pilate "took water and washed his hands
in front of the multitude, saying, 'I am innocent of this Man's
blood' " (27:24). Pilate knew they were shedding innocent blood.
Yet no matter how stubbornly he washed, the stain of his decision would follow him to his grave—a grave that would lead
him face-to-face with the one whose life he washed his hands
of. In a climactic finish to the final trial, Pilate addresses the
crowd.

Now it was the day of preparation for the Passover;
it was about the sixth hour. And he said to the Jews,
"Behold, your King!" (John 19:14)

In a crazed crescendo, the crowd announces for all eternity its
verdict.

"Away with Him, away with Him, crucify Him!" Pilate said to them, "Shall I crucify your King?" The chief priests answered, "We have no king but Caesar." (v. 15) And on the force of those words, Pilate "delivered Him to them to be crucified" (v. 16). The British scholar William Barclay poignantly notes:

> When the Romans had first come into Palestine, they had taken a census in order to arrange the normal taxation to which subject people were liable. And there had been the most bloody rebellion, because the Jews had insisted that God alone was their king, and to Him alone they would pay tribute. When the Jewish leader said: "We have no king but Caesar," it ... must have taken Pilate's breath away, and he must have looked at them in half-bewildered, half-cynical amusement. The Jews were prepared to abandon every principle they had in order to eliminate Jesus.
>
> It is a terrible picture. The hatred of the Jews turned them into a maddened mob of shrieking, frenzied fanatics. In their hatred they forgot all mercy, they forgot all sense of proportion, they forgot all justice, they forgot all their principles, they even forgot God. Never in history was the insanity of hatred so vividly shown.[4]

Standing Alone

The trials are officially over. The jury has rendered its verdict. And innocent blood is fast on its way to being shed.

Pilate washes his hands.

The crowd cheers.

The disciples are nowhere to be found.

Where are you when our Lord's life and reputation hang in the balance? Do you duck down another conversational alley and hide? Do you join in with whatever the crowd is saying or doing? Or do you wash your hands of the whole thing, refusing to take a stand?

It's hard to stand by Christ when some are wishy-washy about Him ... others are shouting "Crucify Him!" ... and still others are deserting Him.

Yet, *He* will never leave *us* ... or forsake *us*. And He will never allow anything or anyone to come between our relationship with Him.

---

4. William Barclay, *The Gospel of John,* vol. 2, The Daily Study Bible Series (Edinburgh, Scotland: Saint Andrew Press, 1956), p. 276.

> For I am convinced that neither death, nor life,
> nor angels, nor principalities, nor things pres-
> ent, nor things to come, nor powers, nor height,
> nor depth, nor any other created thing, shall be
> able to separate us from the love of God, which
> is in Christ Jesus our Lord. (Rom. 8:38–39)
> Strange allies form around the cross—those standing
> *for* Jesus and those standing *against* Him.
> Where do *you* stand?

Living Insights

Study One

Even a casual reading of John 18:28–19:16 gives us the definite feeling of *hurry,* which helps us understand how Christ must have felt during those illegal trials. These verses contain a great deal of action—let's examine it more closely.

- Space is provided below for you to list the action words from the passage we've studied today. Of course, the center of action is the verb. Jot down a dozen key verbs from these verses, and give the meaning and significance of each word.

John 18:28–19:16

Verb _____

Meaning _____

_____

Significance _____

_____

Verb _____

Meaning _____

_____

Significance _____

_____

Continued on next page

65

Verb _____

Meaning _____

_____

Significance _____

_____

Verb _____

Meaning _____

_____

Significance _____

_____

Verb _____

Meaning _____

_____

Significance _____

_____

Verb _____

Meaning _____

_____

Significance _____

_____

Verb _____

Meaning _____

_____

Significance _____

_____

Verb _____

Meaning _____

_____

Significance _____

_____

Verb _____

Meaning _____

_____

Significance _____

_____

Verb _____

Meaning _____

_____

Significance _____

_____

Verb _____

Meaning _____

_____

Significance _____

_____

Verb _____

Meaning _____

_____

Significance _____

_____

Continued on next page

Living Insights

When we understand the trials of Christ, we see how small our own tests are in comparison. All the Savior went through for you and me *before* He went to the cross is amazing. What can we learn from His response to this situation to help us through our times of difficulty?

● Try to come up with some principles from your study of Christ's trials that will help you endure your own.

How I Can Endure the Trials of Life

_____

_____

_____

_____

_____

_____

_____

_____

_____

_____

_____

_____

_____

_____

_____

_____

_____

_____

A Crack in the Rock
John 18:10–18, 25–27

Emerson once said that there is no fear like the fear of being known. Being found out for what we really are is a terrifying experience. Because underneath our veneered smiles and social polish we each hide a fiberboard heart. Full of splinters and sawdust. Rough . . . unattractive . . . cheap.

Peel back the thin facade and look into your heart. Go back into your past. Back to the darkest time in your life. To that act of which you are most ashamed.

It may be something you said.

It may be a habit that once had you in its grip and held you in bondage.

It may be the deepest, darkest secret of your life, known to no one, or perhaps to only a few.

It may be a moral problem that haunts you to this day.

As painful and frightful as it may be, stare at it for a moment. Your face may begin to flush. Your brow may begin to sweat. Your heartbeat may begin to race. But keep staring.

Now imagine that what you're looking at makes the headlines of the morning paper. Or the lead story for the nightly news. Or, worse still, the cover story for "60 Minutes"!

Frightening thought, isn't it?

Doubtless, your first response is that God would never do anything like that. Yet He did.

On numerous occasions, He set in print the inky sins of His people for millions to see. Abraham's lie. Noah's drunkenness and indecent exposure. Moses' rage that left an Egyptian dead. Achan's thievery. The sexual scandals of David, Samson, Amnon, and Gomer. The stubborn defiance of Jonah. And on and on, the headlines are recorded forever in the Bible. For all eyes to see.

With those thoughts in mind, we are now prepared to take a look at the darkest moment in Peter's life. Now we can feel his humiliation. And now, we can realize that each of us has a "Peter's denial" hidden somewhere in our past.

I. Several Significant Events
Peter was known as "the rock." He was the Gibraltar among the disciples. Yet, the rock was not without its cracks. Today, we'll examine the hairline fissures that led to Peter's crumbling under pressure.

A. The surname. When looking at Peter, we can't help but see his underlying potential for greatness, which Jesus saw when Peter's brother Andrew introduced them.

> He brought him to Jesus. Jesus looked at him, and said, "You are Simon the son of John; you shall be called Cephas" (which translated means Peter). (John 1:42)

Unlike what He had done with any other disciple when they first met, Jesus looked closely at Simon. Seeing inner qualities of courage, strength, and loyalty—qualities others might have overlooked—Jesus gave Simon a name that reflected those qualities: Cephas, or Peter, which means "rock or stone."[1]

B. The declaration. Peter's rocklike quality of steadfastness can be seen in John 6:66–69. At a time when people were deserting Jesus in droves, Peter stood resolutely by His side.

> As a result of this many of His disciples withdrew, and were not walking with Him anymore. Jesus said therefore to the twelve, "You do not want to go away also, do you?" Simon Peter answered Him, "Lord, to whom shall we go? You have words of eternal life. And we have believed and have come to know that You are the Holy One of God."

C. The boasting. The last time Jesus and His disciples were together, the Lord revealed that He would leave them (13:33). Peter wrestled with this and then impulsively boasted of his loyalty.

> Simon Peter said to Him, "Lord, where are You going?" Jesus answered, "Where I go, you cannot follow Me now; but you shall follow later." Peter said to Him, "Lord, why can I not follow You right now? I will lay down my life for You." (vv. 36–37)

In spite of how loyal the words appear, they are tinged with pride—a pride, as Proverbs warns, that prefaces a fall (Prov. 16:18, 18:12).

D. The prediction. The crack in the rock is detected by Christ. Thus, Peter's pride leads to a prediction.

> Jesus answered, "Will you lay down your life for Me? Truly, truly, I say to you, a cock shall not crow, until you deny Me three times."[2] (John 13:38)

---

1. *Cephas* is our transliteration of the Aramaic word for "rock." *Peter* is from the Greek *petros,* also meaning "rock."

2. "According to Jewish ritual law, it was not lawful to keep cocks in the holy city, although we cannot be sure whether that law was kept or not. Further, it is never possible to be sure

Footnote continued on next page

In Mark's account, Peter is insistent: " 'Even if I have to die with You, I will not deny You!' " (14:31a).

II. Principles from Peter's Life

Two principles emerge from our study of Peter's life thus far.

A. No one—not even a spiritual rock—is immune to failure. Often, in fact, the rocks are the most vulnerable, according to 1 Corinthians 10:12.

> Therefore let him who thinks he stands take heed lest he fall.

An Eighteenth-Century Peter

Robert Robinson could identify with Peter. He had been saved out of a tempestuous life of sin through George Whitefield's ministry in England. Shortly after that, at the age of twenty-three, Robinson wrote the hymn "Come, Thou Fount."

> Come, Thou Fount of ev'ry blessing,
> Tune my heart to sing Thy grace;
> Streams of mercy, never ceasing,
> Call for songs of loudest praise.[3]

Sadly, Robinson wandered far from those streams and, like the Prodigal Son, journeyed into the distant country of carnality. Until one day . . . he was traveling by stagecoach and sitting beside a young woman engrossed in her book. She ran across a verse she thought was beautiful and asked him what he thought of it.

> Prone to wander—Lord, I feel it—
> Prone to leave the God I love.[4]

Bursting into tears, Robinson said, "Madam, I am the poor unhappy man who wrote that hymn many years ago, and I would give a thousand worlds, if I had them, to enjoy the feelings I had then."[5]

---

that a cock will crow. But the Romans had a certain military practice. The night was divided into four watches—6 P.M. to 9 P.M., 9 P.M. to 12 midnight, 12 midnight to 3 A.M., and 3 A.M. to 6 A.M. After the third watch the guard was changed and to mark the changing of the guard there was a trumpet call at 3 A.M. That trumpet call was called in Latin *gallicinium* and in Greek *alektorophōnia,* which both mean *cockcrow.* It may well be that Jesus said to Peter: 'Before the trumpet sounds the cockcrow you will deny me three times.' Everyone in Jerusalem must have known that trumpet call at 3 A.M. That night it sounded through the city, and when it sounded Peter remembered." William Barclay, *The Gospel of John,* vol. 2, The Daily Study Bible Series (Edinburgh, Scotland: Saint Andrew Press, 1956), pp. 268–69.

3. Robert Robinson, "Come, Thou Fount."

4. Robinson, "Come, Thou Fount."

5. Kenneth W. Osbeck, *101 Hymn Stories* (Grand Rapids, Mich.: Kregel Publications, 1982), p. 52.

> Never forget. That could happen to us . . . no matter how
> solid our faith or what beautiful songs come from our lips.

B. God knows our precise breaking point. Psalm 103 emphasizes that the Lord "Himself knows our frame" (v. 14a). And He knows the stress points on that frame. He knows which parts are subject to metal fatigue, which can be bent, which can be broken. In Peter's case, He knew exactly when that would occur, and under what circumstances. There's a "cock-crow" in all of our lives—a definite time when we can withstand it no longer; and the Lord wants each of us to be aware of our weak points so that we can brace ourselves when that time comes.

III. Process of Denial

Turning to John 18, we'll open the door to four descending steps that lead to the lowest point in Peter's life—his denial.

A. Reliance on the flesh when faced with opposition. Peer carefully into the flickering, torch-lit garden on the night of Jesus' arrest.

> Simon Peter therefore having a sword, drew it, and struck the high priest's slave, and cut off his right ear; and the slave's name was Malchus. Jesus therefore said to Peter, "Put the sword into the sheath; the cup which the Father has given Me, shall I not drink it?" (vv. 10–11)

See anything unusual? A sword in the hands of a fisherman? Jesus Himself has already stated that His followers were not fighters (v. 36). So why the sword? Because Peter is afraid. When we're afraid, we operate in the flesh—trusting in locks and guns and money and all sorts of worldly things. But Christ's kingdom is not of this world. And neither are His weapons (compare Eph. 6:10–20).

B. Reluctance to stand alone when in wrong company. Trailing the captive Christ at a distance, Peter begins to weaken. All it takes for his knees to buckle is a suspicious glance and a probing question from a young servant girl.

> And Simon Peter was following Jesus, and so was another disciple. Now that disciple was known to the high priest, and entered with Jesus into the court of the high priest, but Peter was standing at the door outside. So the other disciple, who was known to the high priest, went out and spoke to the doorkeeper, and brought in Peter. The slave-girl therefore who kept the door said to Peter, "You are not also one of

this man's disciples, are you?" He said, "I am not."
Now the slaves and the officers were standing there,
having made a charcoal fire, for it was cold and they
were warming themselves; and Peter also was with
them, standing and warming himself. (John 18:15–18)

Warming his hands at the same fire that warmed His Savior's
captors! Hardly the place for a disciple. In fact, both testaments
give a clear warning to steer away from relationships that might
cause us to compromise our convictions.

He who walks with wise men will be wise,
But the companion of fools will suffer harm.
(Prov. 13:20)

Do not be deceived: "Bad company corrupts good
morals." (1 Cor. 15:33)

C. **Resistance to be identified with Christ when threat-
ened by the outcome.** Too often we base our decisions on
expedience rather than on eternity. And we end up putting too
much weight on the consequences rather than on principles.
This is what Peter does as he warms himself by the Roman fire.

Now Simon Peter was standing and warming himself.
They said therefore to him, "You are not also one of
His disciples, are you?" He denied it, and said, "I am
not." (John 18:25)

In Matthew's account, the words are even more emphatic: " 'I do
not know the man' "[6] (26:72). If you run with the wrong crowd,
it will be only a matter of time before you will have to declare
your allegiance. And the pressure exerted on Peter at this weak
point exposed, and widened, the crack in his character.

D. **Rejection of the truth regardless of the consequences.**
Fearing recognition, Peter takes a step back from the incriminat-
ing flames of that campfire. But before he can melt into the
shadows, another person pulls at his mask.

One of the slaves of the high priest, being a relative
of the one whose ear Peter cut off, said, "Did I not
see you in the garden with Him?" (John 18:26)

Peter's Galilean accent stood out to these Romans like a Texas
accent in New York City. Matthew's account picks up the dis-
crepancy in dialect.

And a little later the bystanders came up and said to
Peter, "Surely you too are one of them; for the way
you talk gives you away." (Matt. 26:73)

---

6. The word used here for "know" is *oida.* It refers to theoretical knowledge, with the sense
of: "I don't even know who you're talking about."

Peter, rising to the occasion—or should we say "sinking"—lets loose a herd of stampeding expletives that kills the issue underfoot.

> Then he began to curse and swear, "I do not know the man!" And immediately a cock crowed. (v. 74)

Apparently, this is proof enough for these skeptics. They know the truth that a man's " 'mouth speaks from that which fills his heart' " (Luke 6:45b). And certainly this man's heart isn't filled with Jesus. A simple case of mistaken identity caused by the muted shadows of the dying firelight.

IV. Principles from Peter's Denial

Mingling with those shadows are two easily recognized principles that apply to us today.

A. When surrounded by wrongdoers, doing wrong comes easy. Just as it's difficult to walk through a coal mine without getting dirty or to lay down with dogs without getting fleas, so it's difficult to be surrounded by wrongdoers without eventually doing wrong yourself.

B. The first step toward correction is not to act like we're strong but to admit we are weak. Not one of us can condemn Peter. If we were in his shoes, we would have probably done the same. We must also remember, before we wag a critical finger, that the other disciples had abandoned Jesus already. Even though at a distance, Peter still followed Him. True, Peter failed. But he failed in a courtyard where the others dared not set foot.

The Gospel of the Second Chance

"It was like discovering the prize in a box of Crackerjacks or spotting a little pearl in a box of buttons or stumbling across a ten dollar bill in a drawer full of envelopes.

"It was small enough to overlook. Only two words. . . .

". . . Look in Mark, chapter 16. Read the first five verses about the womens' surprise when they find the stone moved to the side. Then feast on that beautiful phrase spoken by the angel, 'He is not here, he is risen,' but don't pause for too long. Go a bit further. Get your pencil ready and enjoy this jewel in the seventh verse (here it comes). The verse reads like this: 'But go, tell his disciples and Peter that he is going before you to Galilee.'

"Did you see it? Read it again. (This time I italicized the words.)

" 'But go, tell his disciples *and Peter* that he is going before you to Galilee.'

"Now tell me if that's not a hidden treasure. . . .

"What a line. It's as if all of heaven had watched Peter fall—and it's as if all of heaven wanted to help him back up again. 'Be sure and tell Peter that he's not left out. Tell him that one failure doesn't make a flop.' . . .

"It's not every day that you get a second chance. Peter must have known that. The next time he saw Jesus, he got so excited that he barely got his britches on before he jumped into the cold water of the Sea of Galilee. It was also enough, so they say, to cause this backwoods Galilean to carry the gospel of the second chance all the way to Rome where they killed him. If you've ever wondered what would cause a man to be willing to be crucified upside down, maybe now you know.

"It's not every day that you find someone who will give you a second chance—much less someone who will give you a second chance every day.

"But in Jesus, Peter found both."[7]

Continued on next page

7. Max Lucado, *No Wonder They Call Him the Savior* (Portland, Oreg.: Multnomah Press, 1986), pp. 93–95.

📖 *Living Insights*

The Bible never flatters its heroes. It presents them shortcomings and all. Early in this lesson, we referred to several Bible characters who were presented with their flaws. For a few moments, let's concentrate on one of these men.

- The following list contains the names of nine Bible characters who had a notable flaw. Pick one person and use the Scripture passage to do further study. Use the space provided to record your observations.

Abraham—Genesis 12, 20
Noah—Genesis 9
Moses—Exodus 2
Achan—Joshua 7
David—2 Samuel 11
Samson—Judges 15–16
Amnon—2 Samuel 13
Gomer—Hosea 1–2
Jonah—Jonah 1–2

Character

_____

_____

_____

_____

_____

_____

_____

_____

_____

_____

_____

_____

_____

Study Two ▬▬▬▬▬▬▬▬▬▬▬▬▬▬▬▬▬▬▬▬▬▬▬▬▬▬▬▬

The people with whom you spend your time play a major role in your spiritual growth. Do you agree with that statement? How does it demonstrate itself in your life? Take a few moments to answer these questions.

1. How has peer pressure affected you in the past?

_____

_____

_____

2. How is peer pressure affecting you now?

_____

_____

_____

3. Why is it difficult for you to stand alone?

_____

_____

_____

4. What would help?

_____

_____

_____

5. *Bad company corrupts good morals.* Do you agree? Why or why not?

_____

_____

_____

6. How has this lesson helped you in this area of struggle?

_____

_____

_____

Death on a Cross
John 19:16–37

A gold cross, hung around your neck or pinned to your lapel, tells the world of your faith. It also symbolizes a certain morality adhered to by Christians. And wearing it often brings a degree of respect from others.

But take that tiny piece of jewelry back in time two thousand years and try wearing it around your neck or on your toga. People would give you puzzled, suspicious looks, thinking you were some kind of lunatic.

For back then, the cross was not a symbol of faith but of failure, not of morality but of lawlessness, not of respect but of unspeakable shame.

Then, the cross was not polished and esteemed. It loomed menacingly on the frayed hem of the city's outskirts, overlooking the garbage dumps. Made of rough-cut timbers and iron spikes, it stood ominously on the horizon . . . a sentry at attention, standing watch for any enemies of the empire . . . a stoic monument that crimes against the state do not pay . . . a splintered vestige of barbarism in the architecture of a renowned civilization.

For Jesus—who had no room in the inn at His birth and "nowhere to lay His head" during His life—the cross was a final place of rest. There He raised His weary, bloodstained head and asked the Judge of the universe not for vengeance, or even for justice, but for mercy on those who crucified and cursed Him. There humanity received a second chance. And an eagerly awaiting Father received His Son.

That is why, for two thousand years, the cross has captured the attention of artists, poets, architects, and yes, even jewelers.

In the cruel brutality, they each saw something beautiful; in the rough-cut wood, something golden.

I. Introductory Information
Before we look at our passage in John, it will help to get a biblical and historical orientation to Jesus' Crucifixion.
A. Scriptural predictions. Some people have the false impression that Jesus was a helpless victim of an insidious plot, a pitiful martyr whose plans were suddenly and unexpectedly terminated by a cross. Such was not the case at all. His Crucifixion had been carefully predicted in the Scriptures.
1. In the Old Testament. Written centuries before Christ, several passages in the Old Testament clearly prophesy of the Messiah's Crucifixion. One of the most prominent is Psalm 22, which tells of hands and feet that are pierced (v. 16b), of bones pulled out of joint (vv. 14, 17), of clothing

divided (v. 18), and of scorning and mocking (vv. 7, 12–13, 17b). Another prophetic text is Isaiah 53. It describes the misery, torture, and pain of God's Servant (vv. 3, 5, 7, 11), the Lord God's planning of the Servant's death (v. 10), and His being crucified with sinners (v. 12).

2. **In the New Testament.** Acts 2:23 explicitly states that Jesus was "delivered up by the predetermined plan and foreknowledge of God." In Acts 3:18, Peter informs us that this predetermined plan was "announced beforehand by the mouth of all the prophets." The evidence is abundant and clear. Jesus was not murdered by an abrupt act of passion; His death was planned by God.

B. Historical orientation. The temporal and geographical information leading up to the Crucifixion will serve to paint the historical backdrop.

1. **The time.** After Pilate's verdict, the governor delivered Jesus over to be crucified (John 19:16, Mark 15:15). This probably occurred between 7:30 and 8:00 in the morning.

2. **The place.** The actual sentencing of Jesus took place at the judgment hall located near Herod's temple. John's account helps us pinpoint the exact place.

> When Pilate therefore heard these words, he brought Jesus out, and sat down on the judgment seat at a place called The Pavement, but in Hebrew, Gabbatha. (John 19:13)

Recent excavations have uncovered what is probably the exact site—a large, elevated, paved area at the northwest corner of the temple site that is part of the Castle of Antonia. Roman soldiers stayed in this castle during Passover to maintain law and order. Doubtless, they looked down from their windows as Pilate presented Jesus to the people. For them, this was great sport, like Monday night football.

II. Christ's Suffering

Step by agonizing step, we'll walk with Jesus through that momentous last day of His earthly life.

A. Scourging of the victim. Although it was unwarranted and unnecessary, Pilate had Jesus scourged (Matt. 27:26, Mark 15:15). There were two kinds of scourging in Jesus' day, Jewish and Roman. Jewish law specified that the victim could not receive more than forty lashes (Deut. 25:1–3). Roman law was not so humane.

> The scourging of Rome was more deadly. It was administered by a trained man, called a lictor. . . . He used a short circular piece of wood, to which were

attached several strips of leather. At the end of each strip, he sewed a chunk of bone or a small piece of iron chain. This instrument was called a flagellum. There was no set number of stripes to be administered, and the law said nothing about the parts of the body to be assailed.[1]

Jesus was stripped and then tied to a low, stone column. In vivid detail, historical biographer Jim Bishop re-creates the gruesome event.

The soldier who performed flagellations for the Jerusalem garrison approached and, out of curiosity, bent down to see the face of the victim. He then moved to a position about six feet behind Jesus, and spread his legs. The flagellum was brought all the way back and whistled forward and made a dull drum sound as the strips of leather smashed against the back of the rib cage. The bits of bone and chain curled around the right side of the body and raised small subcutaneous hemorrhages on the chest....

... The flagellum came back again, aimed slightly lower, and it crashed against skin and flesh. The lips of Jesus seemed to be moving in prayer. The flagellum now moved in slow heavy rhythm.[2]

B. Mocking by the soldiers. But the suffering would not end here. Cruel soldiers, who have circled around Christ's bloody body like vultures, move in to pick at the remains.

Then the soldiers of the governor took Jesus into the Praetorium and gathered the whole Roman cohort around Him. And they stripped Him, and put a scarlet robe on Him. And after weaving a crown of thorns, they put it on His head, and a reed in His right hand; and they kneeled down before Him and mocked Him, saying, "Hail, King of the Jews!" And they spat on Him, and took the reed and began to beat Him on the head. And after they had mocked Him, they took His robe off and put His garments on Him, and led Him away to crucify Him. (Matt. 27:27–31)

In raucous sport, they place a robe on Jesus. But not a long, flowing robe. The Greek term used is *chlamus,* a short cloak worn over the shoulders. Standing there, naked from the waist down, Jesus becomes the object of their vulgar remarks. Each

---

1. Jim Bishop, *The Day Christ Died* (New York, N.Y.: Harper and Row, Publishers, 1965), p. 261.
2. Bishop, *The Day Christ Died,* pp. 261–62.

tries to top the other's joke. Each takes his turn, spitting on Him ... cursing His name ... slapping Him with the reed ... punching His raw chest with their fists. Him, upon whom God would soon bestow a name that was above every other. Him, at whose name every knee would someday bow, of those who are in heaven, and on the earth, and under the earth. Him, before whom every tongue would someday confess that He is Lord (Phil. 2:9–11). But for now, humanity offers this king only spit ... expletives ... and fists.

C. Walking to the site. Criminals were commonly paraded through town, and no exception was made in Jesus' case (Matt. 27:31, John 19:17a). Generally, the victim was surrounded by four Roman soldiers and led by a centurion. As Jesus marched to His execution, He did not carry the entire cross—only the six-foot crossbeam that would later be attached to the larger, vertical post.

> They took Jesus therefore, and He went out, bearing
> His own cross, to the place called the Place of a Skull,
> which is called in Hebrew, Golgotha. (v. 17)

Around His neck hung a 12- by 24-inch placard declaring His crime. This charge was then placed on the cross for all to see: "JESUS THE NAZARENE, THE KING OF THE JEWS" (John 19:19). But the chief priests, notorious for straining at gnats while over-looking the important things, objected to the wording.

> And so the chief priests of the Jews were saying to
> Pilate, "Do not write, 'The King of the Jews'; but that
> He said, 'I am King of the Jews.'" Pilate answered,
> "What I have written I have written." (vv. 21–22)

D. Nailing on the cross. Crucifixion was a barbaric form of capital punishment that began in Persia. The Persians believed that the earth was sacred to Ormazd, the earth god. They felt that death should not contaminate the earth; therefore, crimi-nals were fastened to vertical shafts of wood by iron spikes and hung there to die from exposure, exhaustion, or suffocation. Death was painfully slow and publicly humiliating. Then, vul-tures and carrion crows finished the work. Cicero describes crucifixion as "the most cruel and horrifying death ... incapable of description by any word, for there is none fit to describe it."[3] Jim Bishop, however, again manages to convey the horror.

> The executioner laid the crossbeam behind Jesus
> and brought him to the ground quickly by grasping
> his arm and pulling him backward. As soon as Jesus

---

3. As quoted by William Barclay, *The Gospel of John,* vol. 2, The Daily Study Bible Series (Edinburgh, Scotland: Saint Andrew Press, 1956), p. 291.

fell, the beam was fitted under the back of his neck and, on each side, soldiers quickly knelt on the inside of the elbows. Jesus gave no resistance and said nothing, but he groaned as he fell on the back of his head and the thorns pressed against his torn scalp.

Once begun, the matter was done quickly and efficiently.... With his right hand, the executioner probed the wrist of Jesus to find the little hollow spot. When he found it, he took one of the square-cut iron nails from his teeth and held it against the spot, directly behind where the so-called life line ends. Then he raised the hammer over the nail head and brought it down with force....

Two soldiers grabbed each side of the crossbeam and lifted. As they pulled up, they dragged Jesus by the wrists. With every breath, he groaned. When the soldiers reached the upright, the four of them began to lift the crossbeam higher until the feet of Jesus were off the ground. The body must have writhed with pain....

His arms were now in a V position, and Jesus became conscious of two unendurable circumstances: the first was that the pain in his wrists was beyond bearing, and that muscle cramps knotted his forearms and upper arms and the pads of his shoulders; the second was that his pectoral muscles at the sides of his chest were momentarily paralyzed. This induced in him an involuntary panic; for he found that while he could draw air into his lungs, he was powerless to exhale.[4]

E. **Dying from the pain.** Excruciating pain stabbed the deadweight body that hung on unbending nails. Each movement cut deeper into bone and tendons and raw muscle. Fever inevitably set in, inflaming the wounds and creating an insatiable thirst. Waves of hallucinations drifted the victim in and out of consciousness. And in time, flies and other insects found their way to the cross.

F. **Dealing with the body.** John, the only disciple at the foot of the cross, gives us an eyewitness account of what was done with Jesus' body.

The Jews therefore, because it was the day of preparation, so that the bodies should not remain on the

---

4. Bishop, *The Day Christ Died,* pp. 278–80.

cross on the Sabbath (for that Sabbath was a high day), asked Pilate that their legs might be broken, and that they might be taken away. The soldiers therefore came, and broke the legs of the first man, and of the other man who was crucified with Him; but coming to Jesus, when they saw that He was already dead, they did not break His legs; but one of the soldiers pierced His side with a spear, and immediately there came out blood and water. And he who has seen has borne witness, and his witness is true; and he knows that he is telling the truth, so that you also may believe. For these things came to pass, that the Scripture might be fulfilled, "Not a bone of Him shall be broken." And again another Scripture says, "They shall look on Him whom they pierced." (vv. 31–37)

To speed up death, soldiers would break the victims' legs so they could no longer raise themselves to inhale. But with Jesus, that wasn't necessary. To make sure He hadn't simply passed out, a soldier thrust a spear into Jesus' side.[5]

Make the Cross Your Focal Point

Take a few minutes now to fix your eyes upon Jesus, the author and perfecter of our faith,

> who for the joy set before Him endured the
> cross, despising the shame, and has sat down
> at the right hand of the throne of God. For con-
> sider Him who has endured such hostility by
> sinners against Himself, so that you may not
> grow weary and lose heart. (Heb. 12:2–3)

Now look more intently. Squint your eyes into the darkness of that brutal day. See _how_ He suffered. Peter, who was standing in the distant shadows, strained his eyes. And this is what he saw.

> And while being reviled, He did not revile in
> return; while suffering, He uttered no threats,
> but kept entrusting Himself to Him who judges
> righteously. (1 Pet. 2:23)

---

5. One sign of death is the quick separation of dark red corpuscles from the thin, whitish serum of the blood, here called "water" (v. 34). Normally, the dead do not bleed. But after death, the right auricle of the human heart fills with blood, and the membrane surrounding the heart, the pericardium, holds the watery serum. Jesus' heart must have been punctured with the spear, causing both fluids to flow from His side.

It's hard to look at the shame and suffering Christ endured on the cross. But if we will, our perspective on our own circumstances will never be the same.

If you're weary and losing heart, take a rest. And while you catch your breath, look up the hill . . . up to the one who went before you . . . the one who pioneered the trail so you could follow in His steps (2:21).

🌹 *Living Insights*

Study One ▬▬▬▬▬▬▬▬▬▬▬▬▬▬▬▬▬▬▬▬▬▬▬▬▬▬▬▬

If the trials of Christ produced pain, certainly His Crucifixion produced agony beyond belief. Many times we hurry over the specifics involved in Christ's death, but that is not the case in this lesson. Let's slow down and carefully consider the torture He experienced.

- Let's return to paraphrasing, a study device that will help you get to the heart of the text's meaning and feeling. Write out John 19:16–37 in your own words. This exercise could be one of your most moving interactions with Scripture. Take it slowly and deliberately. Ask God to speak to you as you write.

My Paraphrase of John 19:16–37

_____

_____

_____

_____

_____

_____

_____

_____

_____

_____

_____

_____

_____

_____
_____
_____
_____
_____
_____
_____
_____
_____
_____
_____
_____
_____
_____
_____
_____
_____
_____
_____
_____

Continued on next page

🎋 *Living Insights*

When someone does something special for you, it's customary to express your appreciation. A common way is with a thank-you note. What the Lord Jesus did for us is the ultimate expression of love, and the ramifications are far-reaching. Let's take a few minutes to thank Him.

- In this lesson, we've learned so much about the agonizing death He endured for you and me. Perhaps you want to write a note to the Lord, expressing your heartfelt thanks for all He went through for you.

Thank You, Jesus

_____

_____

_____

_____

_____

_____

_____

_____

_____

_____

_____

_____

_____

_____

_____

_____

_____

_____

_____

_____

A Miraculous Resurrection
John 19:38–20:10

Frank Morison wasn't a man you'd find in church on Sunday morning. Yet you couldn't help but respect him. Although a skeptic philosophically, especially toward Christianity, he was a well-educated Britisher, a lawyer by profession.

His thinking had been shaped by the German critics, Oxford professor Matthew Arnold, and biologist Dr. Thomas Huxley—all of whom openly denied even the possibility of miracles.

In his effort to disprove the historic Christian belief that Jesus was miraculously raised from the dead, Morison began to write a book. Little did he realize that the book he ended up writing would be so radically different from the book he sat down to write. *Who Moved the Stone?* turned out to be a defense of the bodily Resurrection of Christ. In the preface, Morison recounts his intellectual struggle.

> This study is in some ways so unusual and provocative that the writer thinks it desirable to state here very briefly how the book came to take its present form.
>
> In one sense it could have taken no other, for it is essentially a confession, the inner story of a man who originally set out to write one kind of book and found himself compelled by the sheer force of circumstances to write quite another.
>
> It is not that the facts themselves altered, for they are recorded imperishably in the monuments and in the pages of human history. But the interpretation to be put upon the facts underwent a change. Somehow the perspective shifted—not suddenly, as in a flash of insight or inspiration, but slowly, almost imperceptibly, by the very stubbornness of the facts themselves.
>
> The book as it was originally planned was left high and dry, like those Thames barges when the great river goes out to meet the incoming sea. The writer discovered one day that not only could he no longer write the book as he had once conceived it, but that he would not if he could.[1]

In our lesson today, we'll undertake a similar study. And, like Morison, we'll examine the evidence of the Resurrection and allow it to speak for itself.

I. Certainty of the Death
The first thing we will examine is the *corpus delicti*—the actual physical evidence.

---

1. Frank Morison, *Who Moved the Stone?* (London, England: Faber and Faber Limited, 1944).

A. Physical evidence. After looking at the body, the Roman soldiers around the cross rendered the unbiased opinion that Jesus "was already dead."

> The soldiers therefore came, and broke the legs of the first man, and of the other man who was crucified with Him; but coming to Jesus, when they saw that He was already dead, they did not break His legs. (John 19:32–33)

But we have more than simply the testimony of human opinion. Verse 34 furnishes us with undeniable evidence of death—the separation of the dark red corpuscles from the watery serum.

> But one of the soldiers pierced His side with a spear, and immediately there came out blood and water.

This fact is corroborated by John's eyewitness testimony.

> And he who has seen has borne witness, and his witness is true; and he knows that he is telling the truth, so that you also may believe. (v. 35)

B. Procedural evidence. Consider the account of the burial preparations.

> And after these things Joseph of Arimathea, being a disciple of Jesus, but a secret one, for fear of the Jews, asked Pilate that he might take away the body of Jesus; and Pilate granted permission. He came therefore, and took away His body. And Nicodemus came also, who had first come to Him by night; bringing a mixture of myrrh and aloes, about a hundred pounds weight. And so they took the body of Jesus, and bound it in linen wrappings with the spices, as is the burial custom of the Jews. (vv. 38–40)

Now these were friends of Jesus. Had there been the faintest pulse of life in Jesus' limp body, they would have made every effort to resuscitate Him. But instead, they embalmed Him, according to Jewish custom.

II. Silence in the Tomb

Overwhelming evidence confirms that Jesus didn't faint or fall into a coma . . . He died. Then, having been prepared for burial, He was entombed (vv. 41–42).

A. The tomb was sealed. Matthew's account tells us that the body was laid in the cave-like tomb of a rich man named Joseph of Arimathea, who closed the entrance with a large stone (27:57–60). To ensure that the stone would remain unmoved, the Pharisees appealed to Pilate.

> Now on the next day, which is the one after the preparation, the chief priests and the Pharisees gathered

together with Pilate, and said, "Sir, we remember that when He was still alive that deceiver said, 'After three days I am to rise again.' Therefore, give orders for the grave to be made secure until the third day, lest the disciples come and steal Him away and say to the people, 'He has risen from the dead,' and the last deception will be worse than the first." Pilate said to them, "You have a guard; go, make it as secure as you know how." And they went and made the grave secure, and along with the guard they set a seal on the stone. (vv. 62–66)

B. The guards were stationed. The seal consisted of a cord passing across the stone at its widest part and fastened at each end to the rock by sealing clay. Anyone who broke that seal would incur the wrath of the Roman government. The religious leaders helped set the seal, securing the tomb from any interference from the guards. The guards, in turn, prevented interference from the disciples.

III. Separation from the Grave

The time: Sunday morning. The place: the tomb the Pharisees went to such lengths to secure. This is where we'll begin dusting for fingerprints, because something is awry: the seal is broken . . . the stone is rolled away . . . the tomb is empty!

A. The displaced stone. Chapter 20 of John's Gospel introduces us to a new line of evidence.

Now on the first day of the week Mary Magdalene came early to the tomb, while it was still dark, and saw the stone already taken away from the tomb. (v. 1)

The large, circular gravestone covering such a tomb was set on its edge and fitted into an inclined groove, wedged into place by wood or rock. It was not uncommon for such a stone to weigh a ton. Who then could have moved it? It is illogical to assume the guards had, for they would have feared prosecution; or the disciples, because of the presence of the guards. Matthew 28:2 exposes the guilty party.

And behold, a severe earthquake had occurred, for an angel of the Lord descended from heaven and came and rolled away the stone and sat upon it.

B. The empty tomb. The displaced stone revealed an empty tomb. Jesus was gone!

And so [Mary] ran and came to Simon Peter, and to the other disciple whom Jesus loved, and said to them, "They have taken away the Lord out of the tomb, and we do not know where they have laid

Him." Peter therefore went forth, and the other disciple, and they were going to the tomb. And the two were running together; and the other disciple ran ahead faster than Peter, and came to the tomb first. (John 20:2–4)

Only three possible conclusions could have accounted for the empty tomb. First, Jesus could have left of His own account. But this would be impossible if He was still dead. Second, the body could have been taken out by human hands, either those of His friends or of His enemies. If by enemies, what could their motive have been? And if that were true, why did they remain silent when the preaching of Christ's Resurrection hit the streets? They merely would have had to produce the body to nip that rumor in the bud. If the body was taken by friends, how would they have slipped by the guards? Furthermore, it's incomprehensible that those friends would die for the cause of Christ—as all of them, with the possible exception of John, were to do—if it were all a lie. The third conclusion seems to be the only intelligent option: the body left by supernatural means . . . a miracle.

C. The shed graveclothes. Upon coming to the tomb, Peter and John stumbled across more clues.

> And stooping and looking in, [John] saw the linen wrappings lying there; but he did not go in. Simon Peter therefore also came, following him, and entered the tomb; and he beheld the linen wrappings lying there, and the face-cloth, which had been on His head, not lying with the linen wrappings, but rolled up in a place by itself. So the other disciple who had first come to the tomb entered then also. (vv. 5–8a)

Three times in this passage there is a reference to "seeing." The first is in verse 5—he "saw"—and comes from the Greek word *blepō,* meaning "to glance at something." The second is in verse 6—Peter "beheld"—and comes from the word *theōreō,* meaning "to take careful notice." The final occurrence is in verse 8—John followed and "saw." This comes from the word *oida,* which means "to get a mental picture, to realize what has taken place." These two disciples saw the linen wrappings laying on the stone slab like a cocoon from which a butterfly had just emerged. Then all the pieces came together, and it clicked in their minds.

D. The response. What clicked was the trigger of faith.

> And [John] saw and believed. For as yet they did not understand the Scripture, that He must rise again

from the dead. So the disciples went away again to
their own homes. (vv. 8b–10)

Just as with Paul on the Damascus road or Frank Morison con-
ducting his study, the missing piece of the puzzle was found . . .
amid the vacant graveclothes in that empty tomb.

IV. Suggestions for the Living

To live without faith in the Resurrection is to deny the biblical evidence. To die without hope in the Resurrection is to face a barren
eternity. When Frank Morison sat down to sift through the historical
data of the Resurrection, he came with his magnifying glass and his
twenty questions. He came as a skeptical Sherlock Holmes. He also
came facing a barren eternity, without hope. When he finished cross-
examining the biblical evidence, however, he left the courtroom a
convinced man. He concludes his book by stating:

There may be, and, as the writer thinks, there certainly
is, a deep and profoundly historical basis for that much
disputed sentence in the Apostles' Creed—'The *third day*
he rose again from the dead.'[2]

If in your life the jury is still deliberating on whether or not Jesus
rose from the dead, carefully sift through the evidence yourself. After
all, if you're going to be certain about anything, it should be the
Resurrection of Christ. Because, as Paul concludes, "if Christ has not
been raised, then our preaching is vain, your faith also is vain"
(1 Cor. 15:14).

Continued on next page

2. Morison, *Who Moved the Stone?* p. 192.

🎋 *Living Insights*

What is the Resurrection all about? Our study of John's Gospel explains the historical significance in no uncertain terms. But the Resurrection is also the cornerstone of our theology. Let's study another chapter in God's Word in order to understand the doctrinal significance of this great event.

● Why is the Resurrection important? With that question in mind, take a few minutes to read 1 Corinthians 15. Use the chart that follows as a place to record your answers.

Why the Resurrection Is Important 1 Corinthians 15	
Verses	Reasons

In Study One we asked why the Resurrection is important. In this study we want to carry that idea one step further. Why is the Resurrection important *to you?* Have you thought about it lately?

- Use the following space to jot down your musings on the importance of the Resurrection in your life. Write everything that comes to mind. As you do, you may discover deeper feelings you have toward Christ's Resurrection.

Why the Resurrection Is Important to Me

_____

_____

_____

_____

_____

_____

_____

_____

_____

_____

_____

_____

_____

_____

_____

_____

_____

_____

_____

Reactions to the Resurrected Lord
John 20:11–31

You would have expected Christ's followers to rally in faith around the risen Lord. Instead, they recoiled in fear, like little kids huddled around late-night TV watching *The Mummy's Tomb.* They were shocked . . . stunned . . . taken totally off guard. One, in fact, openly refused to believe Jesus was alive unless he could actually see and touch the scars on His body.

For Thomas, seeing was believing. And that, to his discredit. For Jesus said the greater blessing will be bestowed on those who do not see, and yet believe just the same. Their faith is not based on the appearance of things but on the promises of God. It is this type of faith that pleases God and gives glory to Him (see Rom. 4:16–25 and Heb. 11:1–16).

As we study four reactions to the Resurrection, we'll notice some striking similarities to the reactions most people today have toward Jesus Christ. And we'll see how important it is for our faith to be based purely on God's truth and not mixed with anything else.

I. General Observations of the Passage
When Jesus' tomb was found empty, the first fear, voiced by Mary, was that He'd been kidnapped (John 20:2). But after Peter and John investigated the scene, they came to a different conclusion (vv. 8–10). While all the pieces of this puzzling event hadn't fallen into place yet, these two disciples saw enough to get a clear picture: the missing piece was the resurrected Christ. The first sighting of Him occurred early Sunday morning (vv. 11–17); the second, that evening (vv. 19–23); the third, eight days later (vv. 26–29). The people who saw Him were Mary Magdalene (vv. 11, 18), the disciples (vv. 19, 26), and Thomas (vv. 26–28). Another observation of the passage is that the literary structure of each sighting is similar. There is an *appearance* of the risen Christ, a *reaction* to that appearance, and a *statement* made by Christ.

II. Specific Exposition of the Passage
Verses 11–29 of chapter 20 display the four reactions of Jesus' followers.
A. The reaction of Mary: feeling is believing. Mary Magdalene retraces her steps to the tomb alone, drawn by an irresistible desire to visit the place she has last seen her Lord. Troubled and confused, she stands at the mouth of the empty tomb, conversing with angels.

94

> But Mary was standing outside the tomb weeping;
> and so, as she wept, she stooped and looked into the
> tomb; and she beheld two angels in white sitting, one
> at the head, and one at the feet, where the body of
> Jesus had been lying. And they said to her, "Woman,
> why are you weeping?" She said to them, "Because
> they have taken away my Lord, and I do not know
> where they have laid Him." (vv. 11–13)

Maybe it is hazy or foggy on this morning ... maybe tears blur
her eyes ... maybe Jesus is the last person she expects to see.
Whatever the case, she doesn't recognize the risen Lord when
He appears to her.

> When she had said this, she turned around, and be-
> held Jesus standing there, and did not know that it
> was Jesus. Jesus said to her, "Woman, why are you
> weeping? Whom are you seeking?" Supposing Him to
> be the gardener, she said to Him, "Sir, if you have
> carried Him away, tell me where you have laid Him,
> and I will take Him away." (vv. 14–15)

Jesus first addresses Mary as "woman." But when He calls her
by name (v. 16), He immediately comes into focus.

> Jesus said to her, "Mary!" She turned and said to Him
> in Hebrew, "Rabboni!" (which means, Teacher).

Although not explicitly stated, it is implied by this verse that
Mary throws her arms around Jesus and hugs Him with all her
strength. Jesus interrupts this tender moment by giving her a
pressing errand to run.

> Jesus said to her, "Stop clinging to Me, for I have not
> yet ascended to the Father; but go to My brethren,
> and say to them, 'I ascend to My Father and your
> Father, and My God and your God.'" (v. 17)

Convinced and encouraged, Mary returns to the disciples to
announce what she has seen and heard (v. 18). Mary's response
to Christ is typical of a person who is fragile, highly emotional,
unstable, anxious to cling, easily worried, and easily hurt. As
pictured here, Mary typifies a feeling-oriented person with shal-
low roots (compare Mark 4:3–6, 16–17).

B. The reaction of the disciples: seeing is believing.
Abruptly, John cuts to another scene. The room is dark, with
only a flickering oil lamp dancing shadows upon the walls. With
windows shuttered and door barred, the disciples cower in the
shadows ... nails bitten to the nub ... jaws clenched in anxiety ...
heads aching ... throats parched ... tongues clinging to their
mouths.

> When therefore it was evening, on that day, the first
> day of the week, and when the doors were shut where
> the disciples were, for fear of the Jews, Jesus came
> and stood in their midst, and said to them, "Peace
> be with you." (v. 19)

When they first see Jesus, these fearful disciples turn pale as
ghosts (compare Luke 24:37). But with the words "Peace be with
you," a calm settles over their hearts. And when they see who
says these words, they gather around for a closer look.

> And when He had said this, He showed them both
> His hands and His side. The disciples therefore re-
> joiced when they saw the Lord. Jesus therefore said
> to them again, "Peace be with you; as the Father has
> sent Me, I also send you." And when He had said this,
> He breathed on them, and said to them, "Receive the
> Holy Spirit." (John 20:20–22)

These disciples represent a second familiar reaction to Christ;
namely, "seeing is believing."

C. The reaction of Thomas: proving is believing. Thomas
has been tagged the rationalist of the apostolic band. From him
we have our expression "a doubting Thomas." Called Didymus,
meaning "twin," Thomas is mentioned only twice before this
passage: in 11:16, where he says, " 'Let us also go, that we may
die with Him' "; and in 14:5, where he says, " 'Lord, we do not
know where You are going, how do we know the way?' " Thomas,
a bold skeptic who can't live with an unasked question, is your
classic empiricist.

> But Thomas, one of the twelve, called Didymus, was
> not with them when Jesus came. The other disciples
> therefore were saying to him, "We have seen the Lord!"
> But he said to them, "Unless I shall see in His hands
> the imprint of the nails, and put my finger into the
> place of the nails, and put my hand into His side, I
> will not believe." (20:24–25)

Thomas, with his determined "I will not believe unless . . ." attitude, typifies people who will not believe unless Christianity
passes their battery of scientific tests.

D. The reaction of future followers: trusting is believing.
After eight days, Jesus graciously submits Himself to Thomas's
skepticism. And, after doing so, He makes a strong statement
concerning faith.

> And after eight days again His disciples were inside,
> and Thomas with them. Jesus came, the doors having
> been shut, and stood in their midst, and said, "Peace

be with you." Then He said to Thomas, "Reach here your finger, and see My hands; and reach here your hand, and put it into My side; and be not unbelieving, but believing." Thomas answered and said to Him, "My Lord and my God!" Jesus said to him, "Because you have seen Me, have you believed? Blessed are they who did not see, and yet believed." (vv. 26–29)

Note verse 29. Essentially, Jesus tells Thomas: "You've seen and proven, and now you believe. Blessed are those who do not see . . . or feel . . . or prove, and yet believe." This fourth approach to the Christian life is best: trusting is believing. Jesus wants us to rely on Him—without having to feel, see, or prove anything. This leads to the two reasons for John's Gospel: that we may believe and that we may have life.

Many other signs therefore Jesus also performed in the presence of the disciples, which are not written in this book; but these have been written that you may believe that Jesus is the Christ, the Son of God; and that believing you may have life in His name. (vv. 30–31)

III. Practical Applications of the Passage

From the passage we've studied emerge a number of practical applications. First, *subtract facts from faith and you divide your strength.* If your faith isn't grounded in fact, you have a faith without firm foundations. And, like Mary, if you're not careful, you'll find yourself relying on feelings. Second, *add sight to faith and you multiply doubts.* That was Thomas's problem. He had to see for himself. He had to touch the scars. He was living by sight rather than by faith. But Jesus told him: " 'Blessed are they who did not see, and yet believed' " (20:29b). That leads us to the final application: *Mix faith with nothing but the truth and you have life in His name.* When we add anything to the truth, whether it's our subjective feelings or our need for visual confirmation, our faith comes out diluted . . . less potent.

Walking by Faith

In C. S. Lewis's classic *The Screwtape Letters,* Uncle Screwtape, a seasoned devil, corresponds with his nephew Wormwood, a fledgling young devil on his first assignment to earth. In his advice, Screwtape refers to God as the "Enemy" and offers some keen insight into the subject of God's children walking by faith.

He wants them to learn to walk and must therefore take away His hand; and if only the will to walk is

---

really there He is pleased even with their stumbles. Do not be deceived, Wormwood. Our cause is never more in danger than when a human, no longer desiring, but still intending, to do our Enemy's will, looks round upon a universe from which every trace of Him seems to have vanished, and asks why he has been forsaken, and still obeys.[1]

That's what it means to walk by faith instead of by sight or emotion. It is obeying God even when we don't feel like it and even though all visual evidences may be lacking. After all, isn't faith "the conviction of things *not* seen" (see Heb. 11:1, emphasis added)?

Is that how you live? Or do you constantly need your emotions pumped up before you can trust God in difficult-to-believe circumstances? Or do you demand, like Thomas, to see a bigger limb underneath you before you step out in the direction God is prompting you? If so, the ancient prophet Habakkuk has a timely exhortation for you.

Though the fig tree should not blossom,
And there be no fruit on the vines,
Though the yield of the olive should fail,
And the fields produce no food,
Though the flock should be cut off from the fold,
And there be no cattle in the stalls,
Yet I will exult in the Lord,
I will rejoice in the God of my salvation.
The Lord God is my strength,
And He has made my feet like hinds' feet,
And makes me walk on my high places.
(Hab. 3:17–19)

Living Insights

Study One

In no uncertain terms, the writer of the Gospel of John states his purpose for penning his narrative in verses 30 and 31 of chapter 20. Determining the key verse of a Bible book helps us understand why the writer says what he says. Let's explore some other key verses in the Scriptures.

- A key verse is one that explains the book's purpose or summarizes its thrust. Can you think of some key verses for other books of the

1. C. S. Lewis, *The Screwtape Letters* (New York, N.Y.: The Macmillan Co., 1959), p. 47.

Bible? Use the following chart to write down the verses that come to mind. If you can't think of any, pick some small New Testament books (1 John, for example) and discover their key verses.

Key Verses in the Bible	
Book	Verse

Living Insights

Study Two

"Thy Word I have treasured in my heart, / That I may not sin against Thee" (Ps. 119:11). Memorizing Scripture is invaluable because God will help you recall it at the most opportune times.

- Memorize John 20:30–31. Copy it onto an index card and read it aloud over and over. You'll soon see that you need to look less and less at your card! You will have treasured in your heart this wonderful promise from God concerning your life with Him.

Coming to Terms with Your Calling
John 21:1–17

Gone Fishing.

How many times have you wanted to hang that sign on your door? Maybe when there's a lull in business. Maybe when job pressures hem you in and you feel trapped. Or maybe when a wave of nostalgia washes over you one warm summer day and you yearn to go barefoot at the old fishing hole where so many fond memories are pooled.

Maybe those were some of the disciples' thoughts after Jesus died. Perhaps that's why they took the day off and went fishing. The ministry, for all practical purposes, had shut down. Sure, the Resurrection brought a flurry of renewed optimism, but it also raised a number of questions they had no answers for—like, "Now what?"

Perhaps the disciples felt hemmed in by the impending threat of the Roman government. After all, Jesus had warned them that if the world persecuted Him, it would certainly persecute them too.

Perhaps, as they sat by the Sea of Galilee and listened to the rhythm of the waves, they felt their spirits ebbing nostalgically back to the past. When Peter said "I'm going fishing," thoughts of his past came back to him—thoughts of when Jesus first recruited him.

> And as He was going along by the Sea of Galilee, He saw Simon and Andrew, the brother of Simon, casting a net in the sea; for they were fishermen. And Jesus said to them, "Follow Me, and I will make you become fishers of men." And they immediately left the nets and followed Him. And going on a little farther, He saw James the son of Zebedee, and John his brother, who were also in the boat mending the nets. And immediately He called them; and they left their father Zebedee in the boat with the hired servants, and went away to follow Him. (Mark 1:16–20)

For the next three years these fishermen learned from Jesus, observing how He calmed storms, how He walked on water, how He cast His saving net into humanity's sea. But now, in the wake of His death, all was calm, and the disciples returned to their old vocation—back to Galilee and their nets. It is there we find them in John 21.

I. The Disciples Alone

The scene opens on the shores of Galilee's sea, also known as the Sea of Tiberias.

> After these things Jesus manifested Himself again to the disciples at the Sea of Tiberias, and He manifested Himself

in this way. There were together Simon Peter, and Thomas called Didymus, and Nathanael of Cana in Galilee, and the sons of Zebedee, and two others of His disciples. (John 21:1–2)

The disciples find themselves quietly enveloped in melancholy darkness. Few words are spoken. No one knows what to say. One of them skips a rock. Another mindlessly picks up a handful of sand and sifts it through his fingers. Finally, Peter breaks the silence.

Simon Peter said to them, "I am going fishing." They said to him, "We will also come with you." They went out, and got into the boat; and that night they caught nothing. (v. 3)

There was nothing sinful in what the disciples did . . . just negligent. Before they met Jesus, they had a vocation. Now they had more than that; they had a calling. But they were turning a deaf ear to that calling. They were disillusioned . . . confused . . . maybe even feeling sorry for themselves. Ever been there yourself? Are you standing on a similar shore right now, casting nets in some quiet cove, away from the mainstream God has called you to? If so, you may need a visit from Jesus, like the one in the following verses.

II. Jesus and the Disciples

How frustrated the disciples must have felt when time after time their nets came up empty.

A. The manifestation. At the height of their frustration and exhaustion, Jesus quietly appears to the disciples.

But when the day was now breaking, Jesus stood on the beach; yet the disciples did not know that it was Jesus. Jesus therefore said to them, "Children, you do not have any fish, do you?" They answered Him, "No." And He said to them, "Cast the net on the right-hand side of the boat, and you will find a catch." They cast therefore, and then they were not able to haul it in because of the great number of fish. (vv. 4–6)

Barren . . . or Bearing Fruit?

Earlier in the Gospel, Jesus had told the disciples: " 'I am the vine, you are the branches; he who abides in Me, and I in him, he bears much fruit; for apart from Me you can do nothing' " (15:5).

Those words must have echoed in the disciples' minds each time they brought up an empty net. How empty, how futile our lives can be when Christ is left out. When our calling is ignored, we can't sell, we can't teach, we can't counsel, we can't clean house, we can't function fruitfully—

---

period—even in our vocation. The disciples were fishermen by trade, and they couldn't even catch a minnow.

Are your nets coming up empty? Are you burning the midnight oil and getting nothing but burned out? Maybe the Lord is calling to you from the shore. If so, take a minute to listen. He might lead you to the catch of a lifetime!

Imagine the disciples' surprise when they pull up the net brimming with fish, each one a keeper (21:11). The exuberance of the catch causes Peter to pause and remember another time when they were surprised by an incredible catch of fish . . . when Peter first realized who Jesus really was. As he stands there in that little fishing boat, the memory begins to vividly incarnate itself.

> Now it came about that while the multitude were pressing around Him and listening to the word of God, He was standing by the lake of Gennesaret; and He saw two boats lying at the edge of the lake; but the fishermen had gotten out of them, and were washing their nets. And He got into one of the boats, which was Simon's, and asked him to put out a little way from the land. And He sat down and began teaching the multitudes from the boat. And when He had finished speaking, He said to Simon, "Put out into the deep water and let down your nets for a catch." And Simon answered and said, "Master, we worked hard all night and caught nothing, but at Your bidding I will let down the nets." And when they had done this, they enclosed a great quantity of fish; and their nets began to break; and they signaled to their partners in the other boat, for them to come and help them. And they came, and filled both of the boats, so that they began to sink. But when Simon Peter saw that, he fell down at Jesus' feet, saying, "Depart from me, for I am a sinful man, O Lord!" (Luke 5:1–8)

Suddenly Peter's memory is brought into sharper relief by John.

> That disciple therefore whom Jesus loved said to Peter, "It is the Lord." And so when Simon Peter heard that it was the Lord, he put his outer garment on (for he was stripped for work), and threw himself into the sea. (John 21:7)

Rather than wanting the Lord to depart from him, Peter swims the fastest one-hundred-yard freestyle ever seen in order to reach the Savior. Straining at the oars and the net, the others follow Peter.

> But the other disciples came in the little boat, for they were not far from the land, but about one hundred yards away, dragging the net full of fish. (v. 8)

B. The invitation. As Peter and the other disciples reach the shore, they find the meal prepared and the table set. This was no chance meeting but one carefully planned by the Lord.

> And so when they got out upon the land, they saw a charcoal fire already laid, and fish placed on it, and bread. Jesus said to them, "Bring some of the fish which you have now caught." Simon Peter went up, and drew the net to land, full of large fish, a hundred and fifty-three; and although there were so many, the net was not torn. Jesus said to them, "Come and have breakfast." None of the disciples ventured to question Him, "Who are You?" knowing that it was the Lord. (vv. 9–12)

C. The conversation. As in days past, the disciples sit with Jesus, eating and talking together. Their voices murmur across the stretch of deserted beach. Smoke curls above the fire. The radiant heat of the crackling wood begins to chase away the morning chill. It's an intimate moment. Every word that falls from Jesus' lips feeds their hungry hearts. His presence reminds them of that which they had momentarily ignored—their calling. How gracious of the Lord to step into our own sphere of influence—our jobs—and remind us that He still wants us to carry out our calling. To be involved in a vocation *without* a calling is to settle for a life of empty nets.[1]

III. Jesus and Simon Peter

As the sun dawns on that placid sea and the disciples warm themselves by the fire, Jesus opens a recent wound in Peter's life.

> So when they had finished breakfast, Jesus said to Simon Peter, "Simon, son of John, do you love Me more than these?" He said to Him, "Yes, Lord; You know that I love You." He said to him, "Tend My lambs." He said to him again a second time, "Simon, son of John, do you love Me?" He said to Him, "Yes, Lord; You know that I love You." He said to him, "Shepherd My sheep." He said to him the third time, "Simon, son of John, do you love Me?" Peter was grieved because He said to him the third time,

---

1. Daniel's life perfectly illustrates a blending of the two—faithfulness in work (Dan. 6:1–2) and consistency in calling (vv. 3–4).

"Do you love Me?" And he said to Him, "Lord, You know all things; You know that I love You." Jesus said to him, "Tend My sheep." (vv. 15–17)

Three times Jesus asks the same question—one question for each time Peter denied Him. Notice that Jesus doesn't call him Peter, the rock, but Simon. With the name Simon, Jesus takes Peter back to the beginning of their relationship and begins to rebuild the foundation. The first question Jesus asks is, "Do you love Me more than these?" The word *these* isn't identified; it could mean "these men," referring to the disciples, or it could mean "these fish," referring to his vocation. Possibly it refers to both. The Greek word for "love" here is *agapaō,* the highest form of love. Peter's reaction, however, does not include the word *agapaō,* but *phileō,* the word for friendship: "You know I'm fond of You; we're friends." The commission of Christ is clear: "Tend My lambs." In repeating the question, Jesus sensitively drops the phrase "more than these." This takes the pressure off and allows Peter to search his heart to see where the Lord really fits in his life. Again the commission, "Shepherd My sheep." In the final question, Jesus uses the same term for love that Peter has used—*phileō;* "Simon, are you just fond of Me?" Peter is grieved; yet he is honest about where the relationship is: "You know that I am fond of You . . . You know that I have a flawed love." The remarkable thing is that Christ's commission remains consistent: "In spite of that, I *still* want you to tend My sheep. I haven't given up on you. I haven't put you on the shelf."

Coming to Terms with Your Calling

Whether you preach from the pulpit on Sunday morning or pump gas on the corner Monday, God wants to blend your vocation with your calling. Your vocation is special, and your calling is sacred, regardless of whether you wear a clerical collar or a blue collar. No matter what job pays the bills, God wants you to come to terms with your calling and use your job to further His kingdom.

Take a minute to evaluate your priorities: Exactly where does Jesus Christ fit in your Monday-through-Saturday lifestyle? He is asking you today the same question He asked Peter: "Do you love Me more than these?" Do you? If so, you'll find a way to tend His sheep, even while you work.

🐟 *Living Insights*

Tucked away in this final chapter of John is a fascinating conversation between Jesus and Simon Peter. It's been enlightening to watch the relationship between the Lord and Peter mature. Let's review what John records about Peter's life.

- Let's do a biographical sketch of Peter from the Gospel of John. Look for Peter's name throughout the book, and jot down references below. Based on the text, write a summary statement about Peter for each one. Then, if you'd like, feel free to rewrite your sketch of Peter in essay form.

A Biographical Sketch of Simon Peter

Reference _____

Summary _____

_____

_____

Reference _____

Summary _____

_____

_____

Reference _____

Summary _____

_____

_____

Reference _____

Summary _____

_____

_____

Continued on next page

Reference _____

Summary _____

_____

_____

Reference _____

Summary _____

_____

_____

Reference _____

Summary _____

_____

_____

Reference _____

Summary _____

_____

_____

Reference _____

Summary _____

_____

_____

Living Insights

Are you coming to terms with your calling? Is God trying to get
your attention through this study in John? Perhaps until now, God has
been doing all the talking. Maybe it's time for you to take a turn.

- Spend this time talking to the Lord about your calling. As you pray,
  confess your struggles to Him. What hinders you from surrendering
  completely to Him? Have you come to terms with your calling, in
  the fullest sense? Has it touched *every* area of your life? Use these
  questions to guide yourself through a journey of prayer.

"... And What about This Man?"
John 21:17–23

In the wake of Watergate, a crate of books quickly buoyed to the surface. John Dean's *Blind Ambition* ... G. Gordon Liddy's *Will* ... Charles Colson's *Born Again,* just to name a few. Each man looked at Nixon and his administration from a different angle.

But Colson's book is unique. In it, we get a glimpse of intimate details that were not public knowledge, even to the president's closest advisors. It is a moving, personal, transparent account of the inner sanctum of the Oval Office.

The Gospels are similarly written. Each is an eyewitness account from one of Christ's closest confidants. Each has its own particular slant. Matthew, Mark, and Luke look at Jesus through a historical lens, from slightly altered angles.

John, however, is different. He lists no genealogy, and he omits the obvious, familiar events of Jesus' ministry. John's important contribution is taking us behind the scenes to the more intimate moments with Christ— some tender, some trenchant. Today's lesson captures both.

I. Eavesdropping on Jesus and Peter
John 21 forms an epilogue to the Gospel. And like any well-written ending, it is saturated with meaning. From verses 17–23, we'll wring as much as we possibly can. In each section—loving and serving (v. 17), living and dying (vv. 18–19a), lingering and following (vv. 19b–23)—Jesus teaches Peter a significant lesson the disciple has not learned before.

A. Loving and serving.
From our last study we learned that Jesus singled Peter out and asked him three searching questions, each focusing on Peter's love for Him. The questions punctured Peter's heart like a barbed treble hook. You can almost feel the pain from the piercing words: "Do you love Me?" In Peter's mind, he was a failure ... a loser ... a washout. As he sat on the shore listening to Jesus, Peter felt as insignificant as a piece of driftwood about to be fed to the campfire. But when he realized he was not going to be used for kindling but for building Christ's Church, he learned a valuable lesson: *Past failures can be forgiven in love.*

The People God Uses
Have you ever stopped to think about the people God uses to accomplish His purposes? The A-team, right? The heavy hitters—Elijah ... Noah ... Peter ... David ... Jonah ...

Abraham ... Moses. Yet all of them failed; and some, trag-
ically.

When we fail, Satan is quick to run us into the ground
and trample any remaining vestige of self-worth. In fact,
that's what the word *devil* means—"the accuser." He'll
have us call ourselves every name in the book: fool, idiot,
loser, failure.

But love "does not take into account a wrong suffered"
(1 Cor. 13:5b). Jesus doesn't sit in heaven sharpening His
red pencil to jot down every time we fall on our face. Peter
himself tells us, years later, that "love covers a multitude
of sins" (1 Pet. 4:8). And where did he learn that lesson?
Right on that beach where Jesus picked him up and dusted
him off.

You've been there too, haven't you? You've failed Him.
You've fallen flat on your face. When you're down there
with sand in your eyes and mouth, remember: Satan is the
one who's going to kick you while you're down. Jesus will
be there reaching out His hand to pick you up.

B. Living and dying. Still staring at Peter, Jesus informs him of
a contrast that would occur in his life.

> "Truly, truly, I say to you, when you were younger, you
> used to gird yourself, and walk wherever you wished;
> but when you grow old, you will stretch out your
> hands, and someone else will gird you, and bring you
> where you do not wish to go." Now this He said,
> signifying by what kind of death he would glorify
> God. (John 21:18–19a)

The picture Jesus paints in the first part of verse 18 is that of a
self-assured youth, strong-willed, capable, determined, and
independent. But in the latter part of that verse, the picture
changes radically. The strong self-will has been replaced by
submission, a readiness to follow the Savior anywhere, even to
death. In the third volume of Eusebius's *Ecclesiastical History,*
the first-century historian notes that Peter was martyred around
A.D. 61. First, he saw his wife crucified before his very eyes, and
then, with a willing heart, he submitted himself to the cross. But
feeling unworthy to die in the same manner as his Lord, he
asked that he be crucified upside down instead. What a lesson
Peter was to learn as he stood on that shore: *Present lifestyle is
no guarantee of the same future.*

Every day, traders gamble on the stock market, specu-
lating on everything from pork bellies to silver. But in the
flurry of trading in the pits of Wall Street, one thing is
certain:*Nothing* is certain. The Dow can go up one hundred
points as easily as it can go down one hundred. It can crest
or crash in a matter of minutes and leave the investor rid-
ing a speculative roller coaster sure to cause a peptic ulcer.

Just as Wall Street offers no guarantees, so life issues
no insurance policies. As James, the brother of our Lord,
wisely advises:

> Come now, you who say, "Today or tomorrow,
> we shall go to such and such a city, and spend
> a year there and engage in business and make
> a profit." Yet you do not know what your life
> will be like tomorrow. You are just a vapor that
> appears for a little while and then vanishes
> away. (James 4:13–14)

James is not talking about the insignificance of life but
commenting on its ephemeral nature. Like a predawn mist,
our lives, our fortunes, our families, can be burnt away by
the morning sun. Here one minute, gone the next.

Because that's true, James's advice in the following verse
is particularly apropos.

> Instead, you ought to say, "If the Lord wills, we
> shall live and also do this or that." (v. 15)

C. Lingering and following. Peter is learning some timely
lessons. But perhaps Jesus is saving the best one for last, in
John 21:19–23.

> Now this He said, signifying by what kind of death he
> would glorify God. And when He had spoken this, He
> said to him, "Follow Me!" Peter, turning around, saw
> the disciple whom Jesus loved following them; the
> one who also had leaned back on His breast at the
> supper, and said, "Lord, who is the one who betrays
> You?" Peter therefore seeing him said to Jesus, "Lord,
> and what about this man?" (vv. 19–21)

Jesus and Peter are starting to walk away from the group
huddled around the campfire that morning. Looking over his
shoulder, Peter sees John walking behind them at a distance. So
typical of human nature, Peter's mental wheels begin to churn
on the grist of a thought: "And what about John?" Like a char-
coaled ember inflamed by a fanning breeze, an old weakness of

Peter's suddenly flares up. Habitually trying to manage things, Peter sticks his nose into somebody else's business. In doing so, he tries to compare his future to John's. Jesus' response is a terse "mind your own business."

> Jesus said to him, "If I want him to remain until I
> come, what is that to you? You follow Me!" (v. 22)

The lesson comes through loud and clear: *Personal obedience is an individual matter.*

Comparing Brings Confusion

When Jesus asks Peter, "What is that to you?" (v. 22), He is trying to teach the disciple a valuable lesson: God doesn't deal with us on a comparative basis, but on an individual one. He redeems us individually. He rebukes us individually. He rewards us individually.

"Follow Me!" That's the challenge put to Peter. Not to follow John or the rest of the disciples or the majority, but "Me!"

And if you try to follow Jesus while looking over your shoulder to see what direction other Christians are going, sooner or later you're going to stub your toe or stray into a tree.

No, you can only *follow* Him if your eyes are *fixed* on Him—Him and only Him.

II. Summarizing the Applications

Peter learned three lessons on that early-morning Galilee beach. With regard to the past, he learned not to quit. With regard to the future, he learned not to predict. And regarding the present, he learned not to compare. One final thing: verse 23 states that there later arose some confusion about Christ's words to Peter.

> This saying therefore went out among the brethren that
> that disciple would not die; yet Jesus did not say to him
> that he would not die, but only, "If I want him to remain
> until I come, what is that to you?"

Apparently this conversation got garbled in first-century gossip. This leads us to a concluding application: *People often misunderstand God's message.* When that happens, as it inevitably will, don't be concerned. Some things are just between you and God, and some people will never fully understand what He has revealed only to you in the quietness of your heart.

Concluding his book *Born Again,* Charles Colson writes:

> It was that night in the quiet of my room that I made the total surrender . . . : "Lord, if this is what it is all about," I said, "then I thank You. I praise You for leaving me in prison, for letting them take away my license to practice law, yes—even for my son being arrested. I praise You for giving me your love through these men, for being God, for just letting me walk with Jesus."
>
> With those words came the greatest joy of all— the final release, turning it all over to God.[1]

Colson knew that although salvation was a free gift, there was a cost to following Jesus. So did Peter. For him, it would cost his life—a small thing to give up, I'm sure he thought, for all that Jesus gave up for him.

Living Insights

Study One ▬▬▬▬▬▬▬▬▬▬▬▬▬▬▬▬▬▬▬▬▬▬▬▬▬

As we begin to wrap up our time in John's Gospel, we can see how much material we've studied so far. Perhaps it's time to catch our breath by looking back over and reviewing what we have learned.

• You'll find the fifteen previous lesson titles listed below, with space provided for you to summarize in a sentence or two the key *truth* you gleaned from each lesson. Feel free to page back through your study guide and Bible.

Beholding Christ . . . The Lamb of God

Abiding _____

_____

_____

Qualities of a Friend _____

_____

_____

Continued on next page

1. Charles W. Colson, *Born Again* (Old Tappan, N. J.: Fleming H. Revell Co., 1977), pp. 339–40.

The Promise of Persecution _____

_____

Functions of the Holy Spirit _____

_____

Four Words That Keep Us Going _____

_____

Divine Intercession _____

_____

_____

When Jesus Prayed for You _____

_____

_____

Arrest and Trial _____

_____

_____

Rush to Judgment _____

_____

_____

A Crack in the Rock _____

_____

_____

Death on a Cross _____

_____

_____

A Miraculous Resurrection _____

_____

_____

Reactions to the Resurrected Lord _____

_____

_____

Coming to Terms with Your Calling _____

_____

_____

"...And What about This Man?" _____

_____

_____

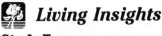 *Living Insights*

Continuing our review, let's turn our attention to some of the applications from these last fifteen lessons. Just how well have we applied all these truths to our lives?

● The list that follows is identical to that in Study One, but now we are asking you to go back over your notes to look for one *application* that really stands out from each lesson. Summarize it in the space provided.

Beholding Christ . . . The Lamb of God

Abiding _____

_____

_____

Qualities of a Friend _____

_____

_____

Continued on next page

The Promise of Persecution _____

_____

_____

Functions of the Holy Spirit _____

_____

_____

Four Words That Keep Us Going _____

_____

_____

Divine Intercession _____

_____

_____

When Jesus Prayed for You _____

_____

_____

Arrest and Trial _____

_____

_____

Rush to Judgment _____

_____

_____

A Crack in the Rock _____

_____

_____

Death on a Cross _____

_____

_____

A Miraculous Resurrection _____

_____

_____

Reactions to the Resurrected Lord _____

_____

_____

Coming to Terms with Your Calling _____

_____

_____

"...And What about This Man?" _____

_____

_____

Many Other Signs . . .
Many Other Things
John 20:30–31, 21:24–25

The End.

With those two words the novelist waves good-bye to the reader. If the book is good, it's a sorrowful parting, and the book is reluctantly closed with a sigh. If the tale has been compelling, the reader walks away from the book a changed person.

When one has finished reading the seventh and final volume of C. S. Lewis's *The Chronicles of Narnia,* it is just such a parting. But the story's end doesn't leave us pining so much for an eighth volume as it creates within us a yearning to be somehow infused into the story itself . . . to be a part of the group and a part of the grand adventure that awaits. Listen to Lewis draw the reader in as he concludes his story.

> And as He spoke He no longer looked to them like a lion; but the things that began to happen after that were so great and beautiful that I cannot write them. And for us this is the end of all the stories, and we can most truly say that they all lived happily ever after. But for them it was only the beginning of the real story. All their life in this world and all their adventures in Narnia had only been the cover and the title page: now at last they were beginning Chapter One of the Great Story, which no one on earth has read: which goes on for ever: in which every chapter is better than the one before.[1]

With these words, the author says good-bye. And with the words covered in today's lesson, our good friend John bids us farewell. It is a tearful parting of author and reader; for the Gospel has been, quite literally, the greatest story ever told.

As we wave good-bye, a yearning wells up inside us—a yearning to be infused into that epic drama as an active participant. As we stand to give our ovations, we long to leave our cushioned seats and take our place on stage with the cast—to be a part of that courageous group and a part of the adventure on which they are about to embark.

I. The Signs He Performed
By the time John writes his Gospel, the end of the first century has arrived. Some sixty years have passed since Jesus died—a long time

---

1. C. S. Lewis, *The Last Battle* (New York, N.Y.: Macmillan Publishing Co., 1956), pp. 183–84.

116

to linger over the photographed memories of His life. With an eye for specific details that would substantiate his purpose, John selects just the right shots for his scrapbook.

A. Stated facts. According to John's own testimony, the account is selective, not exhaustive; the events are actual, not theoretical; the purpose is specific, not vague.

> Many other signs therefore Jesus also performed in the presence of the disciples, which are not written in this book; but these have been written that you may believe that Jesus is the Christ, the Son of God; and that believing you may have life in His name. (John 20:30–31)

B. Illustrated signs. John strings together seven eventful pearls from the life of Christ, and the thread that runs through them all is His deity. The first takes place when Jesus changes water into wine at a wedding in Cana (2:1–3, 7–11). With this miracle, Jesus demonstrates His deity by proving Himself *Master over quality.* The second sign involves the healing of the official's son (4:46–54). Jesus effects the miracle from a distance of twenty miles, thereby proving Himself *Master over distance and space.* The third sign involves the healing of a man who has been sick for thirty-eight years (5:1–9). Jesus shows us in this miracle that there is no problem too old or too established that He can't solve, and in doing so, He proves Himself *Master over time.* In feeding the multitude (6:1–5, 10–14), Jesus convincingly demonstrates that there is no obstacle too large or too widespread for Him to overcome. This establishes Him as *Master over quantity and size.* The fifth sign is found in 6:16–20 where Jesus walks on the water. The Lord quells the disciples' fears with His presence and unquestioningly convinces them that He is *Master over nature.* In 9:1–7, Jesus gives sight to a man born blind, thus showing Himself as *Master over misfortune.* The final and most climactic sign involves raising a dead man from the grave (11:1–6, 14–17, 38–44), dramatically proving Himself to be *Master over death.* In each of these seven miracles, Jesus demonstrates absolute control over all facets of life in which man exerts such little control: quality, distance and space, time, quantity and size, nature, misfortune, and death.

Opportunity Knocking

From time to time great opportunities knock on the doors of our lives—opportunities to exercise faith. But the opportunities that greet us usually come disguised as impossibilities. The only solution to these impossibilities is

---

to introduce them to the Master of the house—the Master
who rules over wind and waves, life and death, heaven and
earth.

Do you have an impossible situation beating down your
door? That knock may *sound* threatening, but it's really
the knock of opportunity—an opportunity to be stretched . . .
and to grow!

II. The Things He Did

Jesus not only stunned the world with incredible accomplishments
that demonstrated His deity, but He served the world with incredible
acts that displayed His humanity as well. John notes this at the
conclusion of his book.

> This is the disciple who bears witness of these things,
> and wrote these things; and we know that his witness is
> true. And there are also many other things which Jesus
> did, which if they were written in detail, I suppose that
> even the world itself would not contain the books which
> were written. (21:24–25)

A. Viewed historically. In the many things Jesus did, He ex-
hibited humility (13:3–5, 12–15), identified with our needs (14:1,
25–27; 16:1, 31–33), submitted to death (17:1–5; chaps. 18–19),
and demonstrated lasting friendship to the disciples (chap. 21).
Even after His work on earth was finished, Jesus lingered long
enough to stabilize those relationships He had built over the
last three and a half years. He was not a distant deity but a
friend who stayed closer than a brother. He visited the disciples
while they were fishing . . . invited them to breakfast . . . accepted
and encouraged Peter . . . and rallied the troops with a "Follow
Me!" reveille. His loyalty and love for those eleven men never
waned. And the effects of what Jesus did for the disciples lived
on, long after He was gone, inspiring them to follow in His steps.
Peter later preached to the same crowds responsible for Jesus'
death and founded the church in Jerusalem. Years later, he was
crucified upside down. James was faithful to the end and was
finally beheaded. Philip labored for Christ until A.D. 54, when he
was scourged, imprisoned, and then crucified. Matthew served
in Parthis and Ethiopia until A.D. 60, when he was bound, covered
with asphalt and oil, and burned to death. Andrew became an
itinerant preacher, ministering especially to the barbaric Scythi-
ans who inhabited what we now know as the Soviet Union. He,
too, was mercilessly beaten and crucified. And Thomas. Remember him? The one we've branded as "the doubter"? He was

118

a missionary to India, where he was imprisoned, tortured by pagan priests, and stabbed to death with a spear. The others as well all died violent deaths in service to their Lord. John was the last to die. He founded churches at cities in a land we know today as Turkey—Smyrna, Pergamum, Sardis, Philadelphia, Laodicea, and Thyatira. He also ministered long at Ephesus. From there he was ordered to Rome, where he was cast into a caldron of boiling oil. He narrowly escaped death, bearing the scars of that ordeal to his dying day. Banished to a life of silent obscurity on the tiny island of Patmos, he there penned three letters, the book of Revelation, and the very Gospel we have been privileged to study.[2] So deep was their love for the Savior, who laid down His life for them, these loyal friends thought nothing of returning the sacrifice.[3]

B. Viewed personally. When Jesus is the subject of our study, all the books in all the world's libraries wouldn't be able to finish the story of His life. When Jesus is the object of our love, our lives change dramatically, and there is no end to the beautiful story our lives could tell. It's one thing to go through a book like John; it's another thing to have the book go through you. It's one thing to have a grasp on John's message; it's quite another to have the message grasp you. As the Gospel of John draws to its denouement, we want Jesus to be not simply the subject of your study but the object of your love. And like the disciples, may you enter into the captivating, adventurous story of life with Christ. And may your story be truly great . . . one that goes on forever . . . in which every chapter is better than the one before!

Continued on next page

2. John's death is clouded in obscurity. Some sources say he died peacefully on Patmos; others say he was hunted down, brutalized, and buried alive.

3. For more information on the deaths of the disciples, consult *Fox's Book of Martyrs,* by John Fox (Grand Rapids, Mich.: Zondervan Publishing House, 1967), pp. 1–5.

Study One

More than likely, many of you completing this study guide are actually completing your third study guide on the Gospel of John. We have worked together through forty-two lessons from this marvelous historical narrative. Let's go back and look at the ground we covered *before* we began this final study guide in the series.

- John 1–14 served as the basis for the first two study guides in this series. Read through those chapters and use the space provided to write in an observation or two from each chapter. Concentrate on doctrinal truths in this study; we'll cover the applications next.

Doctrinal Truths
John 1–14

Chapter 1: _____

_____

_____

Chapter 2: _____

_____

Chapter 3: _____

_____

_____

Chapter 4: _____

_____

_____

Chapter 5: _____

_____

_____

Chapter 6: _____

_____

_____

Chapter 7: _____

_____

_____

Chapter 8: _____

_____

_____

Chapter 9: _____

_____

_____

Chapter 10: _____

_____

_____

Chapter 11: _____

_____

_____

Chapter 12: _____

_____

_____

Chapter 13: _____

_____

_____

Chapter 14: _____

_____

_____

Continued on next page

🌳 *Living Insights*

Since this study guide has concentrated on the last seven chapters of John's Gospel, we've expanded our review to include the first fourteen chapters as well. Let's look at applications that can be made from these texts.

• As you go back and reread John 1–14, pay particular attention to areas of application that you made in these lessons. To help refresh your memory, feel free to consult the study guides that accompany these lessons.

Important Applications
John 1–14

Chapter 1: _____

_____

_____

Chapter 2: _____

_____

_____

Chapter 3: _____

_____

_____

Chapter 4: _____

_____

_____

Chapter 5: _____

_____

_____

Chapter 6: _____

_____

_____

Chapter 7: _____

_____

_____

Chapter 8: _____

_____

_____

Chapter 9: _____

_____

_____

Chapter 10: _____

_____

_____

Chapter 11: _____

_____

_____

Chapter 12: _____

_____

_____

Chapter 13: _____

_____

_____

Chapter 14: _____

_____

_____

Books for Probing Further

"There they crucified Him, and with Him two other men, one on either side, and Jesus in between" (John 19:18).

> The cross stood
>   like a set of scales
>   silhouetted against the Jerusalem sky,
> Its upraised stanchion
>   balancing a crossbeam
>   where love and justice met,
>   where all humanity had been weighed—
>   and found wanting.
> It was there Jesus hung,
>   with outstretched arms,
>   yearning for the world's embrace.
> On either side hung two thieves,
>   teetering between life and death,
>   Heaven and Hell;
> Teetering, until one, at last,
>   reached out in faith:
>   "Remember me when You come into Your kingdom."
> It was the last kind word said to Jesus before He died,
>   spoken not by a religious leader,
>   nor by the disciple whom Christ loved,
>   nor even by His mother standing at His feet,
>   but by a common thief.
> And with the words
>   "Today you will be with Me in Paradise,"
>   that thief was lifted off those weighted scales
>   and into the waiting arms
>   of the Savior,
> And in His arms was carried
>   that day,
>   as promised, .
>   into the Kingdom of God.
> And as they entered, all of Heaven cheered!

—Ken Gire

There is no greater story than the life of Christ. It is epic in all its proportions. Any other story, any other life, pales by comparison.

We hope these studies on the life of our Lord have brought you to the cross, and to your knees. We hope you have seen the Savior a little more clearly, and, as a result, love Him more dearly and follow Him more nearly.

To further your understanding of the cross of Christ, we heartily recommend the following books.

I. A Historical Perspective on the Cross

Bishop, Jim. *The Day Christ Died.* New York, N.Y.: Harper and Row, Publishers, 1957. Tracing Jesus' last day on earth, Jim Bishop re-creates those last hours with reverence, dramatic skill, and a deep understanding of the Roman and Jewish worlds of that time. Its compelling and graphic account will move you.

Maier, Paul L. *First Easter.* New York, N.Y.: Harper and Row, Publishers, 1973. In this fascinating book, replete with photographs, maps, and drawings, the author lays bare the nature of the conspiracy against Jesus; unravels the politics behind the Crucifixion; and documents the Last Supper, the capture at Gethsemane, and the crucifixion process. The book is very readable and reliably researched by a noted professor of ancient history.

Pentecost, J. Dwight. *The Words and Works of Jesus Christ.* Grand Rapids, Mich.: Zondervan Publishing House, 1981. This complete reference book traces the entire life of Christ through the Gospels, explaining the geographical, historical, political, social, moral, and economic conditions that surrounded Him. It is full of quotes from ancient, extrabiblical sources and excellently harmonizes many of the problem passages in the parallel accounts of Christ's life.

II. A Theological Perspective on the Cross

McDonald, H. D. *The Atonement of the Death of Christ.* Grand Rapids, Mich.: Baker Book House, 1985. Written by one of today's finest evangelical historical theologians, this book summarizes the New Testament teaching on the atonement. McDonald expounds and evaluates the views of more than eighty-five theologians on this central doctrine. Although not light reading, it is a good reference to find out where a particular theologian stands on the atonement.

Stott, John R. W. *The Cross of Christ.* Downers Grove, Ill.: InterVarsity Press, 1986. With compelling honesty, the author confronts this generation with the centrality of the cross in God's plan for redeeming the world. At the cross, Stott finds the majesty and love of God disclosed . . . and the sin and bondage of the world exposed. Highly readable and practical, the book is written with penetrating insight, charitable scholarship, and pastoral warmth.

III. A Devotional Perspective on the Cross

Lucado, Max. *No Wonder They Call Him the Savior.* Portland, Oreg.: Multnomah Press, 1986. This outstanding collection of devotional vignettes focuses on the cross—its words, its witness, and its wisdom. It fills in the emotional atmosphere that hung in the air during the last hours of Jesus' life, which is so often missed in a casual reading of the biblical account. Here is a book that will deepen your love for Christ and your understanding of the emotional pain that He, and those who loved Him, endured.

IV. A Personal Perspective on the Cross

Colson, Charles W. *Born Again.* Old Tappan, N.J.: Fleming H. Revell Co., 1977. Christ told Nicodemus in John 3 that unless people are born again, they cannot see the kingdom of God. In this intriguing account of the conversion of President Nixon's top aide, Colson is confronted with the cross of Christ—a confrontation that brings one of the most powerful men in our nation's government to his knees.

Acknowledgments

Insight for Living is grateful for the kind permission granted by the publishers to quote from the following sources:

Barclay, William. *The Gospel of John.* Vol. 2. The Daily Study Bible Series. Edinburgh, Scotland: Saint Andrew Press, 1956.

Bishop, Jim. *The Day Christ Died.* New York, N.Y.: Harper and Row, Publishers, 1965. Permission also granted by International Creative Management.

Lucado, Max. *No Wonder They Call Him the Savior.* Portland, Oreg.: Multnomah Press, 1986.

Insight for Living
Cassette Tapes

BEHOLDING CHRIST ... THE LAMB OF GOD
A STUDY OF JOHN 15–21

In the concluding seven chapters of John's Gospel, the Lamb—Jesus Christ—is on display. After an intimate last supper with His men, He faces the horrors of six illegal trials, scourging, crucifixion, and death. The Lamb is slain ... but He is later raised! These sixteen messages focus our attention on the Lamb of God, who took away our sins.

			U.S.	Canada
BCL	CS	Cassette series—includes album cover	$44.50	$56.50
		Individual cassettes—include messages		
		A and B	5.00	6.35

These prices are effective as of December 1987 and are subject to change without notice.

BCL 1-A: *Abiding*—John 15:1–11
      B: *Qualities of a Friend*—John 15:12–17

BCL 2-A: *The Promise of Persecution*—John 15:18–16:4
      B: *Functions of the Holy Spirit*—John 16:4–15

BCL 3-A: *Four Words That Keep Us Going*—John 16:16–33
      B: *Divine Intercession*—John 17:1–19

BCL 4-A: *When Jesus Prayed for You*—John 17:20–26
      B: *Arrest and Trial*—John 18:1–24

BCL 5-A: *Rush to Judgment*—John 18:28–19:16
      B: *A Crack in the Rock*—John 18:10–18, 25–27

BCL 6-A: *Death on a Cross*—John 19:16–37
      B: *A Miraculous Resurrection*—John 19:38–20:10

BCL 7-A: *Reactions to the Resurrected Lord*—John 20:11–31
      B: *Coming to Terms with Your Calling*—John 21:1–17

BCL 8-A: *". . . And What about This Man?"*—John 21:17–23
      B: *Many Other Signs . . . Many Other Things*—John 20:30–31, 21:24–25

How to Order by Mail

Ordering is easy and convenient. Simply mark on the order form whether you want the series or individual tapes, including the quantity you desire. Tear out the order form and mail it with your payment to the appropriate address on the bottom of the form. We will process your order as promptly as we can.

United States orders: If you wish your order to be shipped first-class for faster delivery, please add 10 percent of the total order amount (not including California sales tax). Otherwise, please allow four to six weeks for delivery by fourth-class mail. We accept personal checks, money orders, Visa, and Master-Card in payment for materials. Unfortunately, we are unable to offer invoicing or COD orders.

Canadian orders: Please add 7 percent of your total order for first-class postage and allow approximately four weeks for delivery. For our listeners in British Columbia, a 6 percent sales tax must also be added to the total of all tape orders (not including postage). For further information, please contact our office at (604) 272-5811. We accept personal checks, money orders, Visa, or MasterCard in payment for materials. Unfortunately, we are unable to offer invoicing or COD orders.

Overseas orders: If you live outside the United States or Canada, please allow six to ten weeks for delivery by surface mail. If you would like your order sent airmail, the delivery time may be reduced. Whether you choose surface or airmail delivery, postage costs must be added to the amount of purchase and included with your order. Please use the following chart to determine the correct postage. Due to fluctuating currency rates, we can accept only personal checks made payable in U.S. funds, international money orders, Visa, or MasterCard in payment for materials.

Type of Postage	Cassettes
Surface	10% of total order
Airmail	25% of total order

For Faster Service, Order by Telephone

To purchase using Visa or MasterCard, you are welcome to use our **toll-free** number between the hours of 8:30 A.M. and 4:00 P.M., Pacific time, Monday through Friday. The number is **1-800-772-8888,** and it may be used anywhere in the United States except California, Hawaii, and Alaska. Telephone orders from these states and overseas are handled through our Sales Department at (714) 870-9161. Canadian residents should call (604) 272-5811. We are unable to accept collect calls.

Our Guarantee

Our cassettes are guaranteed for ninety days against faulty performance or breakage due to a defect in the tape. For best results, please be sure your tape recorder is in good operating condition and is cleaned regularly.

Note: To cover processing and handling, there is a $10 fee for *any* returned check.

Order Form

BCL CS represents the entire *Beholding Christ . . . The Lamb of God* series, while BCL 1–8 are the individual tapes included in the series.

Series or Tape	Unit Price U.S.	Canada	Quantity	Amount
BCL CS	$44.50	$56.50		$
BCL 1	5.00	6.35		
BCL 2	5.00	6.35		
BCL 3	5.00	6.35		
BCL 4	5.00	6.35		
BCL 5	5.00	6.35		
BCL 6	5.00	6.35		
BCL 7	5.00	6.35		
BCL 8	5.00	6.35		
Subtotal				
Sales tax *6% for orders delivered in California or British Columbia*				
Postage *7% in Canada; overseas residents see "How to Order by Mail"*				
10% optional first-class shipping and handling *U.S. residents only*				
Gift to Insight for Living *Tax-deductible in the U.S. and Canada*				
Total amount due *Please do not send cash.*				$

If there is a balance: ☐ apply it as a donation ☐ please refund

Form of payment:

☐ Check or money order made payable to Insight for Living

☐ Credit card (circle one):   Visa   MasterCard

Card Number _____ Expiration Date _____

Signature _____
We cannot process your credit card purchase without your signature.

Name _____

Address _____

City _____

State/Province_____ Zip/Postal Code _____

Country _____

Telephone ( ) _____ Radio Station ___ ___ ___ ___
If questions arise concerning your order, we may need to contact you.

Mail this order form to the Sales Department at one of these addresses:
Insight for Living, Post Office Box 4444, Fullerton, CA 92634

Insight for Living Ministries, Post Office Box 2510, Vancouver, BC, Canada V6B 3W7